BRITAIN IN OLD PHOTOGRAPHS

ROYSTON, CARLTON & MONK BRETTON

BRIAN ELLIOTT

SUTTON PUBLISHING LIMITED

Sutton Publishing Limited
Phoenix Mill · Thrupp · Stroud
Gloucestershire · GL5 2BU

First published 2000

Reprinted in 2001, 2002, 2005

Copyright © Brian Elliott, 2000

British Library Cataloguing in Publication Data
A catalogue record for this book is available from the
British Library.

ISBN 0-7509-2499-3

Typeset in 10.5/13.5 Photina.
Typesetting and origination by
Sutton Publishing Limited.
Printed in Great Britain by
J.H. Haynes & Co. Ltd, Sparkford.

Cover photographs:
Title page: Royston Empire Company Limited was an enterprise formed in the wake of the silent picture age by local farmer and landowner Jonathan Ball who lived on High Street. The Empire and its silver screen became a popular venue on Midland Road, giving hundreds of people opportunity to see the likes of Chaplin and Keaton. It was Ball who had the Palace Picture House built on land a few yards away from the Empire, which from the 1920s concentrated on meeting the considerable demand for dancebands. As a live entertainment centre it was a place where many local marriages had their origins. The building was subsequently used by the Valusta Shirt company. (*Old Barnsley*)

The 1920s could still be regarded as the age of the horse especially in the heart of rural communities such as Monk Bretton. The owner of this vehicle is not known but he must have been what trade directories politely called a 'private resident', that is a person with leisure and means. The entire composition is likely to have been a staged one, even down to the little girl in her best outfit seated on the base of the Cross. Such scenes caught the eye of the buyers of picture postcards as every decent professional photographer fully realised. In 1917 George Hirst was proprietor of the shop shown in the background. Note also the fine haystack of Manor Farm and the gentleman whose curiosity was not perhaps part of the photographer's set piece production. (*Old Barnsley*)

CONTENTS

This vertical aerial view of Royston dates from 1966 at a time when new housing was being developed off High Street and Summer Lane and can be usefully compared with the maps shown on page 8. The form and layout of the present settlement largely evolved from the sinking and development of the Monckton industrial complex just visible in the photograph, in the east of the township. Before about 1890 Midland Road had almost no houses and was known as Senior Lane. This was also the case with regard to Station Road or Overcarr Lane as it was once called. The terraced houses, particularly off the far north side of Midland Road, were built to accommodate the increasing numbers of mainly migrant workers that were attracted to work at Monckton. Planned inter- and post-war housing has clearly made a significant impact on the local landscape, particularly south of the township (eg. Park View, Kirk Cross and Doles estates). The outcome is the emergence of a small but thriving urban area around 'The Wells' crossroads, but with the ancient layout of High Street (with its parallel back lane and village green) and Church Street still easily identifiable. We can also glimpse a landscape that has been worked by man for over a thousand years. The patchwork of shapes, especially south of High Street, are remnants of medieval field systems and more recent enclosures. We can also identify a number of areas of very intensive land-use – between High Street and Back Lane, off Common Lane and Church Street – serving as reminders of Royston's reputation as a market gardening centre. As recently as 1893 there were at least six commercial market gardens and eight farms in the village.

INTRODUCTION

Anyone entering the splendid medieval church of St John the Baptist at Royston, particularly in the good light of mid-morning, should take time to appreciate the magnificent oak timbers of the roof. The carved bosses include the arms of the Priory of St Mary Magdalene de Lund, more popularly Monk Bretton Priory, reminding us of the influence of a small number of brethren and their workmen in celebrating the creation of this fine building. It was the centre-piece of a large parish occupying 13,000 acres of undulating land between the market towns of Barnsley in the south and almost within reach of Wakefield in the north. Apart from Royston itself, the ancient parish consisted of the townships of Chevet, Notton, Carlton, Monk Bretton, Cudworth and Woolley, which had its own chapel of ease. During the first two decades of the nineteenth century the principal settlements continued to be small rural communities ranging from about 300 to 500 inhabitants. By 1840 largely owing to immigrant weavers, the population of Monk Bretton had trebled and the foundation stone of its first church was laid in 1838, forming its own parish in 1843. However, the setting of the pleasant old hill-top village was described during the Feast celebrations of 1859 as 'very picturesque, free from collieries . . .'. This 'freedom' did not last long. A new colliery was sunk in 1867 and was drawing coal by 1870. A few months later Mr Willey celebrated the first coal extracted from his pit at Carlton, and yet another Carlton colliery was working by 1876. Meanwhile the eastern side of Royston township was being transformed by the development of a major mining complex at Monckton. Within a decade Monk Bretton, Carlton and Royston were attracting migrant labour from near and far locations. By the late 1890s all three areas were governed as urban district councils and at the 1901 census Royston and Monk Bretton had populations in excess of 4,000, twice the size of Carlton. Royston was regarded as a small town when it became a part of the County and subsequently Metropolitan Borough of Barnsley during the 1970s.

Despite continued changes the link with the countryside and a sense of community did not disappear, but in the context of very hard times. In 1983 Mrs E. Kaye of Gooder Avenue, Royston, recalled some of the poverty that existed: 'To eke out food my father was, like many others, a poacher. If he was on afternoon shift, he would be out in the local woods until three in the morning. If he brought home a hare it would mean the family had enough for four main meals. . . . Gravy was 'borrowed' from neighbour to neighbour. . . . Next door . . . large consumptive families would borrow the gravy. This, with a large crust of bread, made sure many poor families got at least one good meal a week. . . . Everyone knew everyone and their business. If a neighbour's man was brought home dead [from the pit] and plonked in the front room, my mother and sisters would stay up all night baking scones for the relatives. . . .'

I was born in Royston, in my maternal grandparents' council house at 76 Newtown Avenue, not long after the end of the Second World War. After a few months my parents managed to rent an end-terraced property, in Grays Road, Carlton, near to Wharncliffe Woodmoor Colliery where my father worked. After having waited on the council housing list for many years, the family moved to Monk Bretton, where my father still lives. After completing a course at a College of Education I applied for a post with the West Riding Education Authority and was subsequently appointed as a teacher at the then Royston Secondary Modern School where I spent almost fourteen years, mostly as Head of Geography. I tried to encourage students to be aware of the history of their community and also learnt a great deal myself from this interaction. Researching the history of Royston's ancient parish, and teaching local history classes in Royston and Barnsley, took a great deal of my spare time but was the beginning of an abiding interest that has continued to the present day.

Many people have contributed towards the completion of this book, by loaning photographs and sparing time for me to visit them. Credits are shown in italics after captions to acknowledge their kindness. All other photographs are my own or from my own collection. For general help and encouragement I would particularly like to thank Chris and Pearl Sharp of 'Old Barnsley', Joyce Handley, Megan Elstone, Gaynor Bamford, Kathleen Parks, Rosalie Bailey, Audrey Murdock, Mr and Mrs D. Hindmarsh, Mr and Mrs A. Cook, Mr and Mrs B. Hawkes, Ken Eastwood, Diane Stirland, Margaret Trepczyk, Bill Green, Roy Brown and John Lomas. Simon Fletcher and his colleagues at Sutton have once again been enthusiastically supportive of the project.

Lastly, this collection would not have been possible but for the survival of the excellent work of Royston photographer James L. Wood. It is to his memory that this book is dedicated.

Carlton St John's Football Team (2nd XI) in about 1914, probably in front of the church Sunday school building. The player in the middle of the front row, astride the ball, is team captain Ebenezer Hawkes. Maybe the dog was the club mascot. The team manager and trainer look extremely smart. (*B. Hawkes*)

CHAPTER ONE

ROYSTON WELLS

Two springs once supplied Royston people with water for domestic purposes, but the main public source was sited at the town crossroads known as The Wells (the other was at Guiseley Cottages, near the township boundary with Notton). Unfortunately, by 1892 the town well had virtually dried up because of a leakage that caused 'serious difficulties' to the inhabitants. It was subsequently found that the spring had been diverted 'by building operations', so restoration of the well to 'anything like its old condition' was unlikely. It was then taking eight minutes to fill one bucket. There was also great concern relating to the quality of the water and a potential typhoid epidemic. The eventual outcome, after a local enquiry, was public rejoicing in 1894 when piped water reached Royston via Cudworth. The old town well was redundant and, as we can see in the photograph above, dating from about 1900, was demolished by Septimus Wilson (left) and his workmate: The Wells as a place-name continues into a third millennium.

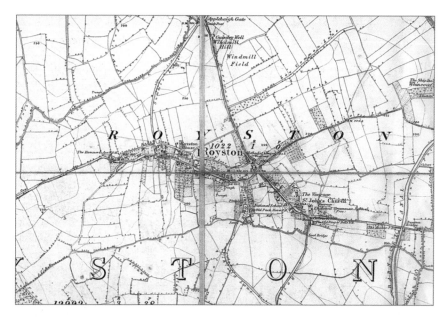

This extract from the first edition (1849–51) of the 6 inch to 1 mile Ordnance Survey map helps us to appreciate what Royston was like as a small rural community before the sinking of nearby collieries. Dwellings are concentrated, linear fashion, in two main areas: between Back Lane and High Street, where the Green with its pinfold stretches across a minor watercourse which formed the southern extent of the township boundary (it was reached via a medieval routeway, Pinfold Lane); and from the town well towards and just beyond St John's church. The market gardening function of Royston is evident from a significant number of orchards and gardens, usually associated with particular properties, though there are 'detached' examples off Senior Lane and Overcarr Lane. The Barnsley Canal's influence can be seen by a small cluster of properties around Whincover and Royston Bridge, with The Ship and The Anchor as public houses sited to serve local as well as passing boat trade.

The 1929/30 (revised 1938) map shows extensive industrial and residential development along what is now Midland Road and Station Road, in a much more familiar settlement plan. Most though not all of the orchards and gardens have been infilled with houses, whilst public services and amenities such as schools, working men's clubs, recreational areas and allotments are well established. The Hammer and Anvil pub at the end of High Street has changed to The Railway in acknowledgement of the close village ties with this form of communication (and Notton station not far away). Anyone living in Royston during the 1920s and 1930s would have been aware of the stark contrast between the old and the new parts of the village. And yet most of the township still consisted of fields – enclosures that had been farmed in various forms for hundreds of years. The relationship between people and the countryside was still a strong part of everyday life.

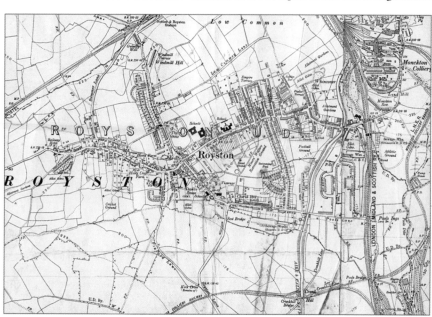

'Animation', where the photographer has captured local people, always adds interest to what would otherwise be dull street scenes. This is the case with this *c.* 1917 example taken at the Wells crossroads, looking towards Station Road. The children at the crossroads appear to be wearing their Sunday best so it was probably an opportunistic appearance by the photographer. The properties on the lower part of Station Road were built during the 1890s, the exception being the Wesleyan (Bethel) chapel of 1803. George Pickering's chemist's shop can be seen at the Midland Road corner (he also provided dental services); next to it is Barclays Bank (open only two days a week); then Alfred Bedford's hairdressers (note the barber's pole) and two general shops.

This view of the Wells crossroads from Church Street, from a postcard sent from Carlton in 1911, is not only enlivened by people but also by everyday transport. A horse and trap turns into High Street and two horse and drays wait outside shops at the bottom of Station Road. The man with walking stick standing in the shadow of Mr Yardley's shopping emporium appears to be keen to be included in the photograph, as do the errand boys by the attractive gas lamp. The corner in front of the imposing Wells House was a popular place to sit and pass the time of day, with public benches provided.

A delightful assembly of children in their Sunday best gather in front of Wells House, *c.* 1910. Some of the adults in the background stand by a piano carried by the horse and dray. The occasion probably related to a chapel anniversary or 'sing'; several of the children are holding what appear to be song sheets. (*Old Barnsley*)

A mid- to late-1930s view of The Wells shows a telephone kiosk and more familiar street furniture, the old gas lamp having been replaced by an electric version of public lighting. One wonders who owned the saloon car with its HL 8604 registration. We also get quite a good view of the small shops at the bottom of Station Road. (*Old Barnsley*)

An advertisement for Hague's chemist shop at Well Hill, *c.* 1955. An interesting piece of history survives relating to the corner of Station Road and Midland Road, where men used to stand and chat on the pavement in front of the chemist's. A policeman is said to have moved them on, presumably for causing an obstruction. But landowner Joseph Oldroyd of the Manor House maintained that they had every right to stand on his property if he gave them permission, going so far as to insert a metal Boundary sign on the pavement, enabling the men to stand on his land as long as they wished. The sign, as can be seen in the photograph below the advert, still survives.

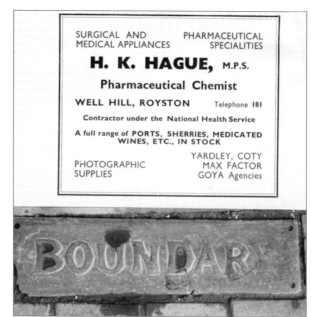

Continuity and change at The Wells. In February 2000 we can now see 'Royston Wells' in large concrete letters as part of the recent urban street improvements to this very busy crossroads, which now merits several pedestrian crossings. Barclays appears to be closed down and the Chettle chemist shop is for sale, but other properties continue to have commercial usage, and the stone buildings have survived in remarkably fine condition. Yet another generation of phone box and street lamp can be seen.

A man rides side saddle on a horse proceeding casually in the middle of Midland Road, and a line of horse and carts await delivery instructions outside Christopher Yardley's grocery/drapery emporium in this superb photograph of the Wells Corner, when it was still the 'horse age'. Horses were shod by blacksmith Arthur Fox at the bottom of the Green. We also have an excellent view of the well-stocked window of the Royston branch of the Globe Tea Company, Walter Neal's printer's and stationer's and Herbert Dickinson's tailor's shop. The boy with the pram adds interest to the scene. (*Old Barnsley*)

An even earlier photograph of The Wells from High Street, the blurred images of some pedestrians a consequence of the camera requiring a long exposure. On this occasion we have a good view of the Andrews family's drapery shop (Manchester House) at the end of Midland Road (now Mick's Carpets). This business was founded by Frederick Andrews in 1891 and appears to have been commercially successful (there were two shops, at 1 and 260 Midland Road), its owner residing at Hafod House, just in view beyond the shop. Just before Yardley's we also get a glimpse of Herbert McKlintock's, where best suits and family jewels could be pawned. (*Old Barnsley*)

Thomas Hinchliffe, with his bowler hat and formidable moustache, must have been a distinctive figure in and around Royston during the 1880s and 1890s. The bundle of letters in his left hand is a clear clue to his occupation: Thomas ran the village sub-post office and shop. Letters arrived from Barnsley at 7.50 am and were dispatched at 5.40 pm.

This photograph of The Wells crossroads was taken by me in 1973 and reminds us of the importance of collecting relatively modern views of familiar areas. There are no signs of any pedestrian crossings apart from at the top of Church Street, and the shops shown here have new occupiers. The 1960s concrete lampstand, as we have already seen, is now replaced by a more graceful example. The man waiting outside the chemist shop is standing within Joseph Oldroyd's old boundary – and the Ford Capri is now a classic car.

The Grove mansion house, off Station Road, was built for Christopher John Yardley in the early 1900s. Later generations of the family included Percy Yardley and his son Norman, who in the 1940s was the Yorkshire and England cricket captain. The house, subsequently used as council offices, appears on the front of *The Official Guide* produced by Royston Urban District Council (when it formed a part of West Riding County Council) during the 1950s.

George Frobisher, bootmaker, churchwarden, councillor and local character outside his cottage, 1 Church Street, photographed by Warner Gothard no later than 1890. This very rare previously unpublished view shows us what the corner of Church Street and Midland Road looked like before this area was commercially developed. Just in view is the double frontage of the new Royston Co-op.

The thirty-second branch of the Barnsley British Co-operative Society opened in Royston in 1889 with John Henry Jackson as salesman. Note the foundation stone which was laid by Thomas Joel Pick on 23 October of the previous year. A second Co-op branch was opened near the end of Midland Road in 1910.

Today (February 2000) the original Royston Co-op building survives, currently in use by Le Scrunsh Studio (a hairdresser's). The old shop front has gone, but the foundation stone, part of the first-floor loading bay, stone-setted yard and a massive stone gatepost remain.

This photograph by Warner Gothard shows the corner of Midland Road at its junction with Church Street and The Wells where three miners are standing, *c.* 1890. It is one of our earliest views of the centre of Royston. The side of George Frobisher's cottage can be seen on the left, and also the stone gatepost and part of the spiked wooden gate of the then new Royston Co-op.

Royston Girls' Brigade (1st Royston Company) march along Church Street and across The Wells crossroads in a celebration of Armistice Day in 1952. The girl with the banner is Gillian Harrison. Others in the photograph include Phyllis and Megan Wooffindin, Norma Standeven, Frances Jackson and Margaret Wood. Also in the marching party is the Company leader Gaynor Bamford (line nearest camera, second right). We also get an interesting view of the commercial properties at the Church Street/Midland Road corner, in particular the Globe Tea Company occupying George Frobisher's old cottage site. (*G. Bamford*)

An early view of Church Street and part of the Wells crossroads, *c*. 1910. The Globe Tea Company were advertising their Christmas Club – as they continued to do, as can be seen in the previous photograph, some forty-two years later.

In contrast, a modern (February 2000) view of the above scene. Wellcroft House, the four-storey building with Palladian-style window on the right corner was opened by Councillor Howard Lavender as recently as 7 September 1999. To some extent the scale of the building, its design (note the 'coach house'-style windows) and materials used echo the Yardley emporium structure that it replaced. Blown Away, Hearts of Flowers and Sweet Dreams now occupy the commercial premises across the road.

Modern photographs help us gain a sense of perspective when viewing collections of older views, and in themselves provide interest. All too often many obvious features are not always noticed, especially amid the noise and rush of passing traffic. Here we can see that after recent road and safety improvements High Street has been noticeably narrowed, almost returning to its former state. From this viewpoint Wellcroft House appears as a somewhat dominating building, perhaps even more so than when Christopher Yardley established his large shop here more than a century earlier.

Another Edwardian view of the top of Church Street. The corner shop was occupied by bespoke tailor Robert Dickinson (compare with page 12) who was pleased to supply made-to-measure 'Mourning Orders'. A boy stands outside Totty Bros, the shop sign indicating the sale of tobacco, books and stationery; they were also newsagents and sold postcards which can be seen on display in the window. Perhaps this photograph was taken on a quiet Sunday afternoon. (*Old Barnsley*)

A page of evocative advertisements from Royston church magazine, 1949.

ROYSTON: CHURCH STREET & HIGH STREET

An Edwardian view of Church Street, looking south. The sign of the old Packhorse Inn can be seen overhanging the narrow street, opposite St John's church. This road, as the inn sign suggests, was part of an important north to south routeway used by travellers from at least the medieval period. Royston Church of England School can be seen on the right of the photograph.

This 1950s view, taken in the opposite (southward) direction from the previous photograph, allows us to look towards The Wells and Station Road. The stone wall of the vicarage garden is on the right.

The old vicarage, 1972. From this viewpoint it appears to be a late Georgian building but, like most buildings of its type, it has a considerable architectural history, stretching from the seventeenth to the end of the twentieth century.

The vicarage as portrayed on an Edwardian picture postcard. In 1684, when the Rev. John Dutton was incumbent, the parsonage consisted of 'A house, garden, fouldstead and Smithy Croft adjoining thereto, being or lying on the north side of the church-yard of Royston and adjoining the church-yard'. Dutton received an annual stipend of £16 13s 4d from the Archbishop of York, supplemented by £15 a year from Lord Londonderry who owned the tithes: not the most generous of livings, but a lot more comfortable than the curate at Woolley who only received £9 per annum. During the long-serving ministry of George Wood (from 1728 to 1782) we have a much more detailed description of the vicarage, which was 'built of stone, and covered with slate containing five rooms, viz. A Kitchen floored with stone and plastered with lime. A Parlour floored with boards and paperd and a small room adjoining the kitchen for an oven and a set pot.' The outbuildings, some of which were thatched, comprised a stable and dovecote, haybarn, cowhouse, swine cote and hen house. It was one of the largest and most comfortable houses in the village. In 1782 the house was extended by the Rev. John Fletcher who added a ground-floor room and two bedrooms. He lived there until his death in 1834. In recent decades the old vicarage has been a private residence, replaced by a modern dwelling, but its survival provides us with a tangible link to previous generations of Royston people.

Royston's magnificent Perpendicular church tower, winter 1995. It was built in the fifteenth century almost certainly under the directions of the monks of the Priory of St Mary Magdalene of Lund (Monk Bretton Priory) who created a most unusual and unique oriel window on the upper part of the west face. Below it are the symbolic heraldic shields and covered unguent pots relating to its Benedictine builders. The window may have been lit as a beacon to travellers since it overlooks an ancient routeway, and the tower would have been the most distinctive landmark for miles around.

When Royston was a small rural community of no more than fifty families, St John's church must have appeared to local people as an immense and dominant building. To a large extent its size and grandeur reflected its importance, Royston being the centre of an extensive parish containing the townships of Chevet, Notton, Carlton, Monk Bretton, Cudworth and Woolley, although the latter had its own chapel of ease. In this Edwardian photograph we have a good view of the old churchyard, so considerably altered during the 1970s. We also have a good picture of the old Packhorse Inn situated just off a bend in the road. Mary Frost had the licence in the 1890s, and during the First World War Joseph Greaves was landlord. George McDonald was there in 1936 and was probably the last landlord prior to its demolition and replacement by the present public house. (*Old Barnsley*)

This modern photograph, taken in January 2000, helps us to make comparisons with the previous scene, which has changed very little over several centuries. Here we can see the 'landscaped' churchyard (in the mid-1970s many old gravestones had been laid flat and bedded in aggregate, the latter now removed and replaced with grass) and the modern Packhorse pub, and next to it a group of flats recently built on the site of the old church school.

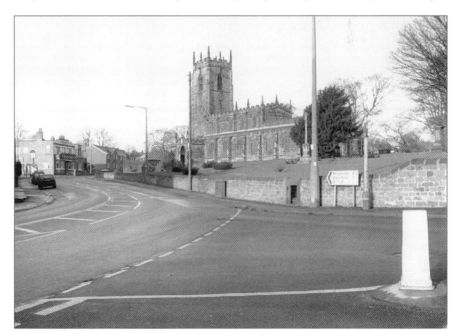

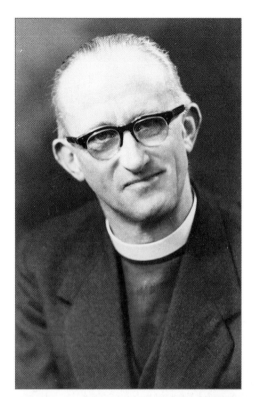

Arthur Paul Leavy, who was instituted as vicar of Royston on 25 July 1952. Many Royston people will have fond memories of this kindly Reverend, who disappeared in the Red Sea en route to Burma where he hoped to work as a missionary priest. (*Rosalie Bailey*)

Below: St John's church choir, probably at Whit, 1966. Back row, left to right: Nicholas Webb (curate), Kenneth Law (vicar), Douglas Such (curate), John Bailey. Third row: Phyllis Chester, Jones, Rita Grearson, George Holland, Alice Hall, Peter Arblaster, Mr Ball, Mossford (?), Len Priestley, Ethel Andrews, Philip Bailey (boy), Paul Green, Rosalie Bailey. Second row: Stephen Williams, -?-, -?-, -?-, -?-, Ward, Val Bailey and Rosalie Ashton. Front row: John Robinson, Robinson, -?-, -?-, Johnson, -?-, -?-, David Parrot/Stratford. (*Rosalie Bailey*)

No. 166. FEBRUARY, 1940.

The Parish Church of S. John Baptist, Royston

MONTHLY MAGAZINE.

VICAR: REV. ROBERT COLLICK, M.A., The Vicarage.
ASSISTANT CURATE: Rev. JACK CATTELL, B.A., 108, Station Road.
READER: Mr. J WRAY, High Street.
CHURCHWARDENS: Messrs. J. Wray and J. P. Buckingham.
SIDESMEN: Messrs. H. Atkinson, F Croft, S. Warren, H. Wood F, Elks, and J, Dawson,
SEXTON: Mr. S Dance, School House, Church Street.

SUNDAYS.—8-30 a m. MATTINS (said).
9-0 a m. SUNG COMMUNION. Also said at 8 a.m. on last Sunday in the month.
11-0 a.m. SUNDAY SCHOOLS.
3-0 p m. EVENSONG.

WEEK-DAYS.—7-30 a.m. HOLY COMMUNION (except Wednesdays, 9 a.m.).
8-0 a.m. MATTINS.
5-30 p.m. EVENSONG, followed by WAR PRAYERS.

BAPTISMS—A week's notice to be given to the Vicar.   CHURCHING OF WOMEN—
BANNS OF MARRIAGE—Notice to be given to the Vicar.   By arrangement.

The Vicar will be in church to hear Confessions on Saturdays at 6-0 p.m.,
or at other times by appointment.

E. CHEESMAN LTD., PRINTERS, 8, MARKET HILL, Barnsley.

The cover of Royston church magazine for the month of February 1940, towards the end of the Rev. Robert Collick's ministry and a few months after the outbreak of the Second World War. Note the War Prayers at Evensong on weekdays.

Royston church interior photographed by Lamb of 80 Racecommon Road, Barnsley; this postcard was used on 14 July 1911. It provides us with a fine and clear image of part of the nave and chancel, looking towards the high altar and east window. The lighting appears to be gas. Note the inscription on the chancel arch.

A similar view, but this postcard by local photographer James Wood was sent on 18 August 1924. There are a number of minor changes to the appearance of the interior, most notably the removal of the inscription on the chancel arch.

This photograph of the chancel and east window of Royston church was taken in the early 1970s, using available light, particularly from the south aisle windows and lady chapel. Note the reticulated tracery of the east window of Victorian glass, and the ogee-headed vestry doorway.

Another picture postcard of St John's, sent from Royston Green and postmarked 15 August 1911. The children by the churchyard wall add interest to the scene.

The Chantry House is probably Royston's oldest surviving vernacular building. The large irregular stone courses of the ground floor contrast with the first-floor addition. It may have been a small single-storey thatched late medieval dwelling. The name originates from the time when the cottage and garden served as an endowment for the chantry chapel in Royston church. The idea was that, in return for money from the endowment, a priest would say (i.e. 'chant') prayers for the departed soul of the provider. This photograph was taken in about 1972, before a new bungalow was built in what was part of the Chantry House garden.

A more distant view of the Chantry House and its new setting, early 1980s. Part of Royston Church School and playground can be seen on the left side of the photograph.

A previous owner of the Chantry House, Mr Taylor, allowed me access for my local history classes during the early 1970s. Mr Taylor often made interesting finds both inside the house and in the garden which had its own well. One of his discoveries was the remains of what appears to be the carved base of a medieval cross-shaft.

The old Chantry House can just be seen in this modern photograph taken in January 2000. A new block of flats now occupies the former school playground, though part of the old playground wall remains. It is always useful for future reference if changes to the setting as well as appearance of our buildings are photographed over a fairly wide time-span, in this instance a thirty-year period.

Another very interesting small house, Rose Cottage, stood just to the north of the Chantry House, which can be seen on the left of this photograph of 1975. Because of the house's modest size its survival, almost anonymous in recent years, was important since it helps us appreciate the kind of cottage dwelling that existed in Royston from at least the middle of the eighteenth century: two ground-floor rooms (parlour or sleeping room and 'house' or living room where meals would also have been originally cooked), and upstairs two chambers and a small loft space. Also note the small two-light windows, which probably once had stone mullions, in the upper storey.

Mr Fox in the back garden of Rose Cottage where he lived for almost sixty years, showing me one of the large roof slates that were superseded by modern pantiles, 1975.

Rose Cottage was a building site when I took this photograph in January 2000, in the process of being completely changed by modern materials. Even the old front doorway has gone. A small part of the cottage garden wall remains, but perhaps not for long.

The old Royston Grammar School (white building) and its outbuildings, early 1970s. The school, which took boarders, closed in the early 1900s. In this view we also have a glimpse of 'work in progress' in the churchyard, when many gravestones were moved and laid flat amid pebble aggregate. The old school dormitory building had fallen into decline in subsequent years but remedial work now appears to be forthcoming.

ROYSTONE GRAMMAR SCHOOL,
NEAR BARNSLEY.

ESTABLISHED BY KING JAMES I., A.D. 1607; UPON THE FOUNDATION OF JOHN FORMAN, VICAR, A.D. 1450.

Head Master - Mr. JOHN WALTER RHODES, B.A., Trinity College, Cambridge.

It will be the earnest desire of the Master to give to all boys committed to his care a sound and practical education, which may qualify them, as may be desired, for Agricultural or Mercantile pursuits, or for the learned professions.

Instruction is afforded in the principles of the Christian Religion, according to the doctrines of the Church of England; in the Greek and Latin Languages; the principles of Algebra and Mathematics; Reading, Writing, Arithmetic, and Mensuration; Sacred and Secular History; Geography and English Literature and Composition.

Where it is desired, additional instruction can be given in French, Drawing and Vocal and Instrumental Music.

The buildings are apart from the village, in a most healthy and agreeable situation. Each boarder has a separate bed; and as the number is limited the greatest possible care and attention can be paid to their personal comfort, health, general demeanour, and moral conduct.

LESSONS.

Great care is taken that the boys may thoroughly understand the lessons they are required to learn; and frequent vivâ voce examinations are given, in order to discover the particulars in which a pupil may be deficient, so that such defects may be remedied.

PRIZES

Are given Annually to the best proficients in the several subjects; and a daily register is kept of each boy's conduct and progress, so that each lesson has its influence in the distribution of Prizes at Midsummer.

LIBRARY.

In order to cultivate a taste for reading among the pupils, during their leisure hours, a Library has just been established, (1858), and though small at present it is hoped that through the liberality of friends it will before long be sufficiently large to furnish them with a varied supply of interesting and useful information.

Small contributions of books, or money for the purchase of books, will be gratefully received by the master.

GAMES.

Every possible inducement is held out to the boys to practice such games as are calculated to improve their health and exercise their reasoning powers.

TERMS.

DAY SCHOLARS residing in the Parish are admitted to the privileges of the School on payment of TEN SHILLINGS per Quarter, in advance.

	Per Annum.
Day Scholars, not residing in the Parish	4 Guineas.
Daily Boarders, including School Fees	10 "
Weekly Boarders, ditto	25 "
Half-Yearly Boarders, under 12 Years of Age, ditto	30 "
Half-Yearly Boarders, above 12 Years of Age, ditto	35 "

The last two charges include Washing. There are no extras except for Books and Medical attendance.

The Boarders are never allowed to leave the Grounds without permission.

A QUARTER'S NOTICE OR A QUARTER'S PAYMENT IS EXPECTED PREVIOUS TO THE REMOVAL OF A PUPIL.

Advertisements extolling the curriculum and character-building virtues of Royston Grammar School were regular insertions in local newspapers from the late eighteenth century, and printers were commissioned to produce information sheets that would be given or sent to prospective parents. Here is a typical example from 1858. Most local families could not afford to send their children to the school, as the fees were too high.

This photograph, showing a cluster of contrasting properties at the bottom of Church Hill at its junction with Church Street/Royston Lane, probably dates from about 1930 when Horace Walker held the licence at the Old Ring of Bells. During the First World War Thomas Wombwell was publican, and in the early 1890s Mary Ann Roodhouse. Percy Hodgson was landlord in the mid-1930s and H. Kyte in the 1950s. We also have a good view of the old Grammar School in its early usage as a private house, with washing on the clothes line. Next to the Ring of Bells is St John's View, and on the hillside is another substantial and then modern detached house. (*Old Barnsley*)

The old canal or bridge house, 79 Church Hill, *c.* 1973. Probably dating from the early 1800s with a later extension, it was strategically sited by a canal bridge and housed a succession of waterway employees. Across from it stood the the Hope and Anchor, a bargees' inn. Mrs Mary Thawley held the licence in 1893. Former inhabitants of the house include the Smith family, head of household Joseph being described as 'canal foreman' in the 1881 census. Joseph left the house on his retirement in 1921, the next occupants being James Hedley and his family. The canal bridge was lowered to road level and the canal culverted in about 1960. I visited the house in the early 1970s courtesy of Mrs Hedley, who had then lived there for thirty-three years.

Looking across the landscaped churchyard towards St John's View, the Ring of Bells Hotel and the Ace Ballroom, a former cinema near the township boundary, *c.* 1980. The ballroom was subsequently converted into the Bethel Community Church. The land between the Ace and the pub was often used as a venue by visiting funfairs.

ACE CINEMA :: ROYSTON

Telephone: Royston 79.

PROGRAMME FOR FEBRUARY

Feb. 2nd (2 days)—RICHARD GREENE and PATRICIA MEDINA in "DON'T TAKE IT TO HEART." (u)

Feb. 4th (2 days)—FRANCHOT TONE and JANET BLAIR in "I LOVE TROUBLE." (a).

Feb. 7th (2 days)—RON RANDELL and MURIEL STEINBECK in "SOUTHERN CROSS." (u).

Feb. 9th (2 days)—ROBERT DONAT and DEBORAH KERR in "PERFECT STRANGERS." (a).

Feb. 11th (2 days)—LANA TURNER and RICHARD HART in "GREEN DOLPHIN STREET." (a).

Feb. 14th (2 days)—SANDY POWELL, DAN YOUNG and BETTY JUMEL in "CUP-TIE HONEYMOON." (a)

Feb. 16th (2 days)—PETER LORRE and ROBERT ALDA on "THE BEAST WITH FIVE FINGERS." (a).

Feb. 18th (2 days)—IDA LUPINO and WAYNE MORRIS in "DEEP VALLEY." (a).

Feb. 21st (2 days)—MARGARET O'BRIEN and ROBERT PRESTON in "BIG CITY." (u).

FEB. 23rd (2 days)—WALLACE BEERY and TOM DRAKE in "ALIAS A GENTLEMAN." (a).

Feb. 25th (2 days)—JEANETTE MACDONALD and JOSE ITURBI in "THE BIRDS AND THE BEES." (u) In Technicolor.

Feb. 28th (2 days)—ANNA NEAGLE and MICHAEL WILDING in "THE COURTNEYS OF CURZON STREET." (u)

TWO HOUSES MONDAY AND SATURDAY AT 5-45 AND 8-30 P.M.
ADULT MATINEES MONDAY AND THURSDAY AT 2 P.M.
OTHER EVENINGS ONE HOUSE AT 7 P.M.
SPECIAL PICTURES FOR SATURDAY CHILDREN'S MATINEES AT 2 P.M.

Programme for the Ace Cinema for February 1949. The cinema attracted large numbers of people from Carlton as well as Royston, and the Saturday morning children's matinee was extremely popular during the 1950s.

This interesting cottage, 13 High Street (opposite the former chapel), was built in 1801 and functioned as a small farm. In the 1840s its occupier was John Ball. It was obtained by the local council, and my maternal grandmother recalled (in the 1960s) paying her rent there many years earlier. Before its unfortunate demolition in the early 1970s it was used by the council for the storage of building materials.

This view was taken by me in about 1973, looking towards High Street from land that would have once been associated with the '1801' High Street cottage, its rooftop just visible behind overgrown vegetation and a large shrub. Note the range of farm buildings on the right, also demolished in the 1970s. The barn had a datestone of 1835. This was a very interesting group of buildings in the old part of the village.

Royston's ancient Green, from High Street, 1970s. The Pinfold Estate seen in the distance was one of the first post-war council housing areas, made up of a hundred 'steel houses' and eighty brick houses of various sizes. The houses had electricity and bathrooms, though toilets were still outside. I can just remember the village smithy being demolished at the bottom of the Green in the 1950s.

Holly Croft Farmhouse (34 High Street), pictured here in the early 1970s, is one of the few eighteenth-century buildings that have survived demolition along High Street.

Part of High Street as it appeared in about 1950. Note the small wooden shop on the right where Saturday pennies could be spent on Mrs Wray's sweets. People that lived along High Street from the Green to Lee Lane were sometimes referred to as 'Top-Enders'.

Royston's Manor House, photographed in 1973, shortly before its demolition. It was a fine and imposing building with interesting outbuildings, and within living memory was associated with the Oldroyd family.

Another sad loss to Royston was the demolition of Home Farm, architecturally and historically one of the most important buildings in the village. The house had a late Georgian front which had been added to a much older structure of at least 1650 (note the two-light mullions at the Oakwood Road side of the building). I completed a photographic survey whilst its demolition was in progress in July 1973. This photograph was taken in January 1972.

Home Farm was replaced by a small development of chalet-style houses, as can be seen in this photograph taken in January 2000. Part of the stone boundary wall and a lintel datestone are now distant reminders of the old building.

Part of the great barn at Home Farm during its demolition, the roof slates already removed. The steps at the brick gable on the right side were once used for access into a dovecote. Note the massive timbers that supported the structure. The barn appears to have built at different periods: the above shows a more recent phase, but the middle area included remnants of cruck framing, revealed during demolition and hitherto hidden by later stonework.

Detail of a massive tie-beam in the middle part of the barn. It is clearly a re-used piece of timber which had considerable carving on it, including a circular motif enclosing a cloverleaf design, almost certainly taken from a high-status structure. There are some parallels with the original monastic roof carving in Royston church. It would not be out of the question for this and other timbers to have been obtained from the dissolved Priory at Monk Bretton. The other timbers are more modern but still fixed by pegs. The infilling is of hand-made brick, crudely mortared.

Part of High Street and the junction with Oakwood Road, 1976. Building work on the Home Farm site can be seen starting in the foreground, all the outbuildings having been demolished. Across towards High Street we can see another eighteenth-century barn, which has now gone.

Maltlkiln Farm, High Street in the early 1970s, when its owner, Mr Lappage, allowed me to visit this interesting late seventeenth-century building. Although much altered it was one of the principal farmsteads of Royston. In the days when many houses as well as inns brewed their own beer, the supply of barley and malt was a commodity in much demand.

The Railway Hotel, when it was a 'Tennants house' and when its stone roof tiled outbuildings were still intact, *c.* 1972. The bay windows at the front of the building were added sometime after 1911. It was formerly the Anvil and Hammer pub; Edward Wallace held the licence in 1893 and was probably succeeded by Fred Moxon. In 1936 the landlord was Charles Potter.

The Railway Hotel as a 'Whitbread house' mid-1970s. Stabling and former coaching areas can be seen, though some outbuildings have clearly been demolished.

Members of the Royston & District Horticultural Society pose for their photograph outside the Railway Hotel, 1911. Notice the array of caps and hats! Back row, left to right: A. Bayliss, T. Walters, F. Proctor, G. Griffiths; Second row: G. Jackson, W. Andy (reading!), T. Hold, R. Chapman, H. Woodcock, J. Peckett, W. Senior, S. Burton, W.H. Brooks; Front row: Mr and Mrs Moxon, R. Hill, A. Rogerson, A. Griffiths, M. Woofindin, G. Sommers. The photograph also helps us to appreciate the old appearance of the inn.

New houses on Station Road. This development of about fifty brick dwellings, and also another seventy-two on Newtown Avenue, was built by the council during the 1930s. They have changed relatively little in appearance. The schoolchildren add interest to the scene. (*Old Barnsley*)

Few photographs survive relating to the hamlet of Old Royston. This picture postcard example was posted in Royston on 4 August 1912 by W. Bagshaw, who informs 'Dear Friends' (at Killamarsh, near Sheffield) that 'ours [house] is against the wood'. He or she also describes that 'it has been our Feast this last week end'. The cottages were probably occupied by railway workers.

The Cross Inn, Summer Lane, when it was a John Smith's establishment in the early 1970s.

For several generations a butcher's has functioned from a small corner shop at the junction of High Street and New Street. The butcher on this early photograph (holding a dog) is probably Hiram Woofindin who was in business from at least 1893. The present-day occupants are McQuillan & Sons. By the mid-1930s there were at least eleven butchers in Royston, including Harold Shaw of 10 High Street who had been in business for a century.

Ten shilling notes being given out by Royston Old Age Christmas Fund, 1930s. (*D. Hindmarsh*)

CHAPTER THREE

MIDLAND ROAD & MONCKTON

What appears to be a Whit procession, headed by the Salvation Army band, makes its way along Midland Road, c. 1919. There is much of interest in this scene: we get a glimpse of George Bilham's corner shop (no. 158), the small walled gardens at the front of the terraced houses and the wide pavements in contrast to the narrow street. All the children wear hats or caps, whilst among the spectators there is a mixture of Sunday best and working clothes, several of the women wearing shawls. In the distance there is a horse and trap. J.L. Wood must have taken this photograph from the window of an upstairs room or attic. (Old Barnsley)

Midland Road Mixed Public Elementary School was erected in 1896 with places for 883 children, with a new infants' wing added in 1902. The master at about the time this photograph was taken (*c.* 1915) was J.R. Timpson BA, with Miss Sykes as mistress and Miss Caroline Witty as Infants' mistress. (*Old Barnsley*)

A contrasting view, January 2000. The Junior School closed in the early 1980s, replaced by a new building on High Street. The site of the school now includes a small supermarket and pharmacy. A small part of the original school wall and most of the trees remain.

Formerly known as Senior Lane, Midland Road developed as the main thoroughfare for shopping and services from about 1890 to 1920. In the distance and facing the mud-strewn street are the Palace Cinema (built in 1914), and next to it (separated by Victoria Road) the Empire Picture Theatre, then Alf Jones's baker's shop, George Cheetham's draper's shop (with bike outside), Royston Post Office (W.J. Powell, who can just be seen reaching for a sale item through the window) and the 'Cash Chemist' (Pickering's) offering 'Pure Drugs at Cash Prices'. This photograph by J.L. Wood dates from about 1920. (*Old Barnsley*)

Midland Road from a similar viewpoint, January 2000. The family furnishers F. Mount took over the properties formerly occupied by Powell's post office and the Cash Chemists in the early 1950s; the Empire is now Burberry's (and earlier Valusta Shirts) factory; and the old Palace Cinema is a snooker hall/video hire shop. All the buildings are extant but their usage has either changed or, in the case of smaller shops, they have been abandoned.

PALACE, Royston.

Tel.—
Royston 12.   **Programme for June**

June   2—Whit-Monday—Matinee at 2-30   Two Houses at 6 and 8-40 p.m.
,,   3—Whit-Tuesday—One House only.
              Maureen O'Hara, Jeff Chandler in FLAME OF ARABY (U) Tech. also
              William Powell, Rosemary De Camp in TREASURE OF LOST CANYON (U) Tech.
,,   4—2 days   Clifton Webb, Anne Francis, William Lundigan in ELOPEMENT (U) also
                                                              THE GORILLA (A).
,,   6—2 days   Anthony Steel, Dinah Sheridan in WHERE NO VULTURES FLY (U) Tech.
,,   9—2 days   Joseph Cotten, Barbara Stanwyck in THE MAN WITH A CLOAK (U).
,,   11—2 days   Montgomery Clift, Elizabeth Taylor in A PLACE IN THE SUN (A).
,,   13—2 days   Douglas Fairbanks, Yolande Donlan in MR. DRAKES DUCK (U).
,,   16—2 days   Alan Ladd, Deborah Kerr in THUNDER IN THE EAST.
,,   18—2 days   Victor McLaglan, Nan Grey in EX-CHAMP (U) also
                         Mark Stevens, Robert Douglas in TARGET UNKNOWN (U).
,,   20—2 days   Yvonne De Carlo, Edmund O'Brien in HIGH VERMILLION (A) Tech.
,,   23—2 days   Shelley Winters, Gary Merrill, Michael Rennie in
                                PHONE CALL FROM A STRANGER (U).
,,   25—2 days   Joan Fontaine, Ray Milland in SOMETHING TO LIVE FOR (A) also
                                                              JUNGLE FLIGHT (U).
,,   27—2 days   Kathryn Grayson, Ava Gardner, Howard Keel in SHOW BOAT (U).

Matinee—Monday and Thursday at 2-30 p.m.
TWO HOUSES ON SATURDAYS — 6 p.m. and 8-45 p.m.
(CHILDRENS MATINEE EVERY SATURDAY AT 2-0 p.m. SPECIAL PICTURES)

The programme for the Palace Cinema for June 1952. The entertainment strategy appears to have been to show films in rapid (mostly two-day) succession. In this respect the Palace 'competed' with its sister cinema, The Ace on Royston Lane; but this was a time when variety was essential since many people enjoyed 'going to the pictures' two or three times a week.

The former Palace Cinema was purpose-built in 1914 with an 'art deco' façade, not complimented by the cream and blue paintwork of today. It continued showing silent films during the First World War and 1920s. Jim Watson was the regular pianist, apparently noted for playing *The Entry of the Gladiators* as a prelude to the opening of the screen curtains. The writer's memory of the palace relates mainly to the 1950s, attending Saturday afternoon matinees with friends, especially to see cowboy films – which had us galloping all the way to Carlton (apart from diversions to defend ourselves from Indian attacks).

In this photograph taken further eastwards along Midland Road other shop premises can be seen. Just before a side street (North Road), at no. 159, is Melias Ltd (grocers), then the small pawnbroker's shop (no. 161) owned by David Haigh (previously by Herbert McKlintock) and Wallace Laidlaw's newsagency (no. 163). Opposite the parked car is Mark Westnedge's double-fronted footwear and clothing shop known as The Central (nos 165–7) and, with a dog outside, Robert Harwood's butcher's shop (no. 169). Most of these business had been established about the First World War period. (*Old Barnsley*)

Who would have thought that Westnedge's old-established family shop would be transformed into a 'Tone 'n' Tan' establishment, as shown in this January 2000 view. Such is the pace of change that the redundant brick chapel just in view facing traffic on the extreme right of the photograph was demolished two weeks later.

Brothers Harold (aged sixty) and Eric Westnedge (seventy-three) outside The Central in 1983. The business was founded in 1902 by their father Mark Westnedge. Eric recalled a time when 'everyone shopped in the village' and 'were paid out at the pits and all walked past our shops on the way home, often calling for goods'. Both brothers were born behind the shop.

The old canal bridge in the distance at the end of Midland Road and a 1936 postmark helps to date this photograph to the early 1930s, since the bridge was replaced in 1934. It was still a time when to cycle and walk in the middle of the road was a safe activity. Here most properties are residential, though commercial premises and a former shop can be seen on the right of the picture. (*Rosalie Bailey*)

Construction work in progress on and under the stone Midland Road bridge during 1933, with men and boys peering over, looking in the direction of intrepid photographer James Wood. An empty canal boat can be seen moored to the left of the bridge. Keel boats loaded with wood pulp en route from Goole to Marsden's Paper Mill at Old Mill, Barnsley, obviously had to negotiate the bridge with great care, lowering their sails. Bargees of horse-drawn vessels also had to approach the bridge with considerable dexterity, otherwise the animal (taking the strain) might take an unexpected and dangerous plunge into the canal.

The canalside Ship Inn was strategically sited at the Whincover end of Midland Road, convenient for both boat traffic and the fast-developing colliery. This photograph was taken in about 1974 when it was a John Smith's public house. There is no inn sign other than the Courage cockerel stuck incongruously over the central entrance. Daniel Greenfield was one of its first publicans, resident in the 1890s. Jesse Scull held the licence from the First World War through to the 1930s. The modern concrete headgear of part of the New Monckton Colliery complex can be seen in the background. This formed part of an expensive NCB modernisation programme but the pit closed in late December 1966, leaving about 1,600 miners drawing their wages for the last time. My father (born in 1917) remembers his father and other Monckton colliers meeting outside the pub to divide up their weekly earnings at a time when wages were paid to teams of workers. Dad also had to make sure, if at all possible, that his father came straight home!

One of several photographs published by Wood of the new canal bridge, probably taken just before or after its official opening on 26 June 1934. On the approach of boat traffic Mr Scott, the bridgemaster, was able to stop road vehicles passing over the bridge with the barriers that can here be seen in place whilst the bridge was raised, allowing any vessel to pass without obstruction underneath. With the decline of canal traffic during the 1950s, Royston's new bridge had a short operational life.

The official opening of Royston's new canal bridge attracted a great deal of public interest and celebration, as can be seen by the attendant crowd and display of flags and bunting. George Griffiths, centre, was one of the VIPs cutting the tape. A newly elected MP (for the Hemsworth Division), Mr Griffiths was a former Monckton miner and trade union official who had served for many years on the Royston Urban District Council. Henceforward, the bridge often had Griffiths appended to its name.

A view of the redundant bridge, 1974. Despite its uniqueness as a piece of interesting local industrial archaeology the bridge was demolished shortly afterwards.

The site of the former Royston lift bridge is hardly recognisable today (February 2000). Landscaping has been such that even the course of the old canal is not apparent to the casual visitor. Only the concrete posts of the former wire safety fence remain *in situ*. Tall metal chimneys of the modern Monckton Coking Company complex (RJ Budge Group) can be seen in the distance and Morgan's corner shop (before The Ship, see page 57) is disused.

Looking northwards towards Old Royston, from the Midland Road canal bridge: a view of the Whincover area, *c.* 1969. The terrace properties on the left have long gone and today the canal is a far less obvious landscape feature. For many families the canal was part of an open-air playground (see the little girl approaching the water's edge), but one that occasionally had tragic consequences.

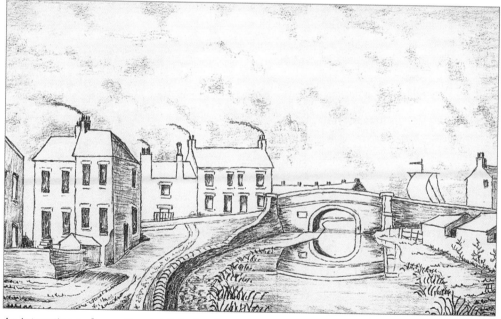

An interesting and evocative sketch by local man Tom Ashton, looking south, towards the old stone bridge over Senior Lane, and showing a keel boat in full sail approaching Whincover. (*Rosalie Bailey*)

An equally interesting 1950s photograph of the end of Midland Road and the Monckton area. A steam train can be seen passing along the Midland Railway, with a pit spoil heap in the background. A bus stops at Royston Midland station and another has just passed under the railway bridge. Just beyond the bridge is the stationmaster's house and beyond that the Monckton Club and Institute, which had been opened by Mr Ellison, MD of the Monckton Group of Collieries, on 18 May 1907. For many years this building and its grounds were the venue for both regular and occasional sporting, musical and social events. (*Old Barnsley*)

A hearse approaches the old railway bridge and Monckton Hill in about 1972, when part of the station buildings was used as a club: note the Tetley brewery sign.

A modern (January 2000) view of the Midland Road/Monckton area provides us with interesting comparisons with the previous two photographs. Some landscaping, including tree planting, has softened the shape of the old pit heap, but the Monckton Institute has gone. The Ship now has a sign showing a canal narrow boat, although such vessels were not usually common on this waterway.

Almost deserted platforms at Royston station, *c.* 1909. The men sitting on wicker baskets may have had a long wait before they loaded their racing pigeons. In the background are Monckton Colliery complex and what appears to be part of Monckton Row, a group of three terraces (long demolished) built for mineworkers just south of the pit, on the left side of Lundhill (see page 60). Washing can be seen on a clothes line stretched across the yard of one of the houses – the wind appearing to be in a favourable direction on this occasion. (*Old Barnsley*)

This is certainly part of Monckton Row, as sketched by Thomas Ashton, with the chimneys of the pit in the background. In the foreground is the running track of the Monckton Club and Institute. There was a popular gymnastics and athletic section, though the football club was the most thriving activity, a number of players progressing to football league clubs. (*Rosalie Bailey*)

The bewhiskered stationmaster and staff at Royston pose for J.L. Wood's camera in 1923. The stationmaster was Charles A. James, who may have succeeded Arthur Snow.

This aerial view of the eastern part of Royston township was taken in the summer of 1966, when the colliery (but not the coking and chemical plant) ceased production. It demonstrates the considerable size of the industrial complex to the west of Lundhill Lane and its massive impact on the local landscape. The arrow points to Monckton Row, referred to on page 59.

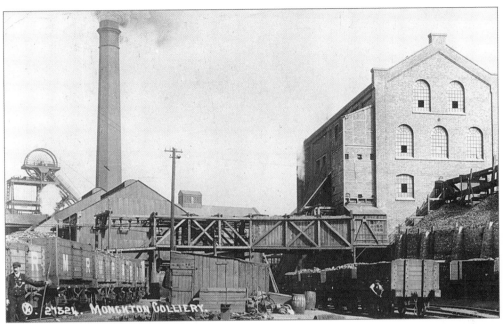

The Monckton Collieries and Coking Plant and Monckton Main Coal Company Ltd was registered in 1874 (Monckton being the family name of the Lords Galway). A clay mill was built for brick-making in 1875, and was soon producing 25,000 bricks a year. Shaft sinking began in 1875 and the first shift commenced two years later, the first sales at 4s 3d per ton of household nuts. Experiments in coke making progressed in 1878 and in 1879 work started on the erection of twelve beehive ovens, soon increased to forty-two. From 1901 additional shafts were sunk when the company registration changed to New Monckton Collieries Ltd under the chairmanship of Viscount Galway and A.S.F. Assinder as manager. The pit attracted large numbers of migrant workers from the Black Country, to such a concentration that part of the village became known as 'Little Staffordshire' and a distinctive local dialect developed, still present when I taught at the secondary school in the early 1970s. By the Second World War Monckton was employing 4,000 men. (*Old Barnsley*)

This early photograph shows two workmen standing on top of the pit cage at Monckton colliery. The person standing on the left may be assistant manager Mr G. Buckle.

Tom Ashton (left) and Willie Thorpe in the winding engine house at Monckton, *c.* 1930. (*Rosalie Bailey*)

Out-of-the-way working-class houses are likely to have been neglected by early photographers and in modern times cleared as slums, for development. Here part of a terraced row called Strawberry Gardens (marked but not named on 6 inch to 1 mile maps), photographed in about 1972, not long before the houses were demolished. My great-grandparents, Albert Winter (1865–1934) and his wife Eliza Ann (née Rogerson, 1870–1920), lived in the end house towards the end of their married life. Albert was a master boot and shoemaker by trade. There was an orchard of mature pear trees just to the left of the photograph, stretching towards Low Common Lane.

Another view, this time showing the gable end and backs of Strawberry Gardens. There was a gap between the slightly later and larger properties in the foreground and the smaller terrace group in the distance. It is the former group that was shown in the previous photograph. Note the zinc baths hung outside several of the houses.

A fine pencil sketch executed by Thomas Ashton of a headgear and engine house at New Monckton colliery in 1945. (*Rosalie Bailey*)

In 1936 James L. Wood produced an award-winning portfolio of photographs relating to New Monckton Collieries, some of which were produced in David Joy's compilation *Life in the Yorkshire Coalfield* (Dalesman, 1989). This and the next photograph (part of an unpublished series) were taken by Wood more than ten years earlier. They relate to building work in progress at the Monckton Coke and Chemical Plant and, as we can see, are of a very high quality. This superb example, dated 13 November 1922, shows men working on the roof of one of the main new buildings. (*RJB Mining/Monckton Coke and Chemical Company*)

A more panoramic photograph by James Wood, showing building work taking place on a considerable scale, July 1922. (*RJB Mining/Monckton Coke and Chemical Company*)

Workers at Monckton Coke and Chemical Company in 1908 at a time when this end of Royston must have resembled the Klondyke of North America. One wonders how many men on this photograph were migrants. The men are gathered in front of a building known as The Ram, which housed machinery that expelled the coke out of the ovens. The bearded man is believed to be James Wood (not the photographer of the same name), who lived at Strawberry Gardens. (*RJB Mining/Monckton Coke and Chemical Company*)

The Monckton Coke and Chemical Co., Ld.

I, the undersigned, hereby agree with The Monckton Coke and Chemical Co., Ld. to faithfully serve the said Company from the date hereof, and to Obey and Fulfil the orders of the Manager of the said Company, and also to obey and fulfil the Rules and Regulations of the said Company, a copy of which I now acknowledge to have received, and that I will serve the Company at their works as regularly as the state of trade, shortage of fuel, interruption from accidents, repairs to works, non arrival of wagons, will from time to time permit, and the said Company agree to engage the undersigned as a By-Product Coke Oven Worker.

It is also agreed that the Company is empowered but not bound to make advances or supply to me any of the articles, matters and things, or to perform any work or to make any payments specified and set out in the next succeeding paragraph, and to deduct from any wages from time to time due to me the amount of such advances and the value of any such articles, matters and things, or work, or the amount of any such payments, together with the rent (if any) of any house or land occupied by me.

Things to be supplied, &c.:—Coal, Fuel, or Timber—Tools—Check Weigh Fund—Inspection—House Rent—Subscription to Permanent Relief Fund—Colliery Club and for Medical Attendance—Voluntary Levies—Institute—National Health and Unemployment Insurance.

This Contract to be terminated by seven days notice in writing on either side.

Signature   *Charles. Stone*

Residence   *Taylors Yard, Staincross*

Occupation   *Salt House Whizzerman & Salt Packer*

Age   *30*

Whether Married or Single   *Married*

Where last Worked   MONCKTON COKE & CHEMICAL Co. Ltd.

Key No.   *865*

Date of Signing on   *Jany 3rd 1927*

Date of Leaving   *24. 1. 1964*

*Signed for and on behalf of **The Monckton Coke & Chemical Co., Ltd.**

T. W. ADAM, General Manager,

By   *A Jarvis*   , duly authorised

Charles Stone, my maternal grandfather, spent most of his working life in the employ of the Monckton Coke and Chemical Company Ltd, retiring at the age of sixty-eight in 1964. Here is his contract of employment for 1927 (though he probably worked for the company a number of years earlier), in which he has the amazing occupational name of 'salt house whizzerman and salt packer'. For many years Charles and his wife Mary lived in Newtown Avenue, Royston.

Charles Stone ascending the steps of the Salt House at the Monckton Coke and Chemical Company, *c.* 1964. Charles was born in rural Dorset in 1896, the eighth son of a policeman. As a young man he moved away from home and, following service during the First World War, worked as a horseman at Holly Croft Farm. He subsequently married Mary Winter of Staincross and found employment at the Monckton Coke and Chemical Company. Charles and Mary lived at Doles Cottages, High Street, and then at 76 Newtown Avenue.

Royston Joiner's Tragic Death

FELL DOWN PIT SHAFT.

H.M. INSPECTOR AND HOISTING DANGERS.

The District Coroner (Mr. C. J. Haworth) sat with a jury at the Ring o' Bells Inn, Royston, on Friday last, to inquire into the circumstances surrounding the tragic death of John Gothard (49), colliery joiner, of Rivelyn, Church Hill, Royston, who fell down the new shaft which has been sunk at the New Monckton Collieries, on the previous Wednesday. There were also present Mr. G. Cooke (H.M. Inspector of Mines) and Mr. John Davies (representing the Power Section of the Transport Workers' Union).

Alfred Hancock, engineer at the colliery, of Green Mount, Havercroft, said he was in charge of the mechanical working of the sinking of the new shaft, and at about 1.45 p.m. the previous Wednesday he was on the pit top along with deceased. Witness was about six yards away when he heard a noise, and, turning round, found deceased had disappeared down the shaft. About five or six men were working there, and most of them were looking down the shaft.

DEPTH OF SHAFT.

The Coroner: What is the depth of the shaft?—One hundred yards; but there were about thirty feet of water at the bottom.

As far as you were concerned you don't know what knocked him down?—No.

Did you see what had fallen?—Yes, a snatch block.

Witness said the block had come from a rope suspended above the men.

HOISTING ARRANGEMENTS.

The Inspector: Don't you think it was risky to work immediately below where men were pulling up the snatch block?—Witness: No.

Do you think it is safe to stand beneath something which is being pulled up?—We always work below them when sinking a shaft. I didn't think it was wise to stop the job, because hoisting is always being carried on.

The Inspector: But I think it is.

The Coroner: Wouldn't you think it safest not to stand in the way of anything being hoisted? You wouldn't walk under a ladder where a painter is using a pot. You would walk round, not because you were superstitious, but because the paint pot might fall, although it would be only once in a hundred times.

A Juryman: Was the snatch block in motion at the time?—Yes.

Then it would be possible for it to catch a girder?—Yes.

The Coroner: What distance would it fall before striking the man?—About twenty feet.

KNOCKED DOWN BY SNATCH BLOCK.

Patrick Costello, a pit sinker, of 327, Midland road, Royston, said he was just going on the pithead when he heard a shout and saw the snatch block drop. In its descent it caught a girder, and then bounded to hit deceased on the back of the head knocking him down the shaft. Deceased had been standing on the top platform, and there was one several yards lower down. He must have passed between the side of the shaft and this platform. Witness later went down to recover

An unusual accident occurred at the New Monckton Collieries in 1928 when John Gothard, aged forty-nine, fell down a new shaft during sinking operations. The report of the accident and inquest report appeared in some detail in the *Barnsley Chronicle*.

Although Monckton collieries ceased production after 1967 a new drift mine was opened on the eastern side of the hill, opened by NCB chairman Derek Ezra. Worked on the American system of retreat mining, the two drifts produced exceptionally high volumes of coal for use by the Central Electricity Generating Board. However, output was so great that the life of the new mine was restricted to ten rather than twenty or more years, and mining finally came to an end. Across the road, the Monckton Coke and Chemical Company, developed by private enterprise during the reign of Queen Victoria, survives into the twenty-first century, now part of the RJB (Budge) Mining Group.

CHAPTER FOUR

CARLTON

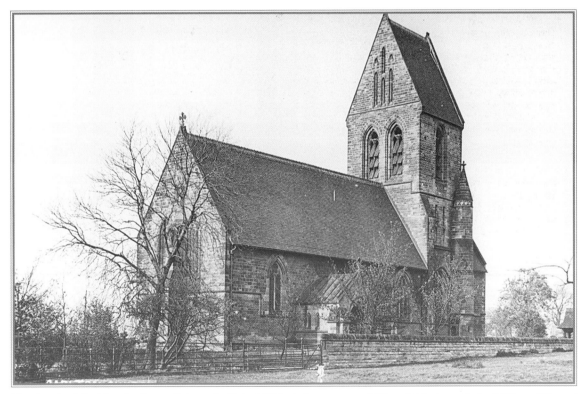

The church of St John the Evangelist was built in 1879 at the expense of Edward Montagu, Earl of Wharncliffe, and dedicated to his father, John, who had died in 1855. The tower with its tall and steep saddleback roof makes a most distinctive landmark, the whole design executed by G.E. Street of London and described by Nicholas Pevsner as 'one of the grittiest of his churches'. The large crucifix and war memorial of white Portland stone, sited at the east end of the churchyard, is missing from this view which dates from the Edwardian era. (Old Barnsley)

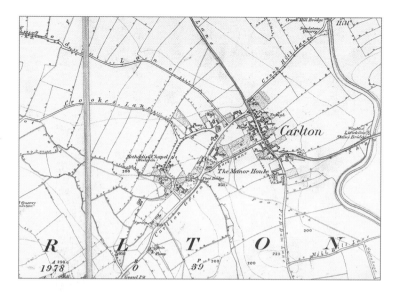

The 1851 '6 Inch to 1 Mile' OS map shows Carlton as a small rural community, its principal properties stretched along a main north–south street and thoroughfare, but partly enclosed by dual prongs of an elongated Back Lane, in fact a fairly typical Anglo-Saxon settlement form for our area. The meandering course of the Barnsley Canal almost exactly mirrors the 175 ft contour to the east of the village. The only named buildings are the first Methodist chapel built in 1842 and Manor House (Farm).

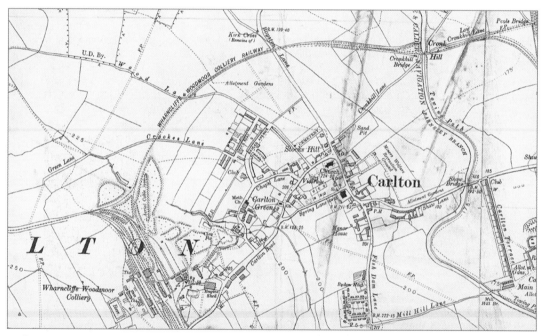

In the 1929 and 1938 editions of the same map the development of Wharncliffe Woodmoor Colliery to the west of the village and, just out of view, Carlton Main Colliery to the east, clearly has had impact on the landscape of the old township. Carlton Terrace, a long row of houses, forms a distinct mining community serving the eastern colliery, whilst colliers' houses developed by the pit owner Willey (for example on Carlton Road) and by other opportunistic private landlords are evident, particularly north of Chapel Lane. Another small but separate housing development, locally known as Sticky Top, can be seen at the junction of Fish Dam Lane and Mill Hill Lane. St John's church, the Methodist chapel and Spring Lane School are now the dominant public buildings, but we should also notice three areas of 'allotment gardens', a village 'club' and Miners' Welfare recreation ground. The 'Midland line' (just out of view) takes a direct north–south route east of what is now called the Barnsley branch of the Aire and Calder Canal, but there are rail links to both village collieries. Yet despite all the changes the ancient layout of Carlton remains extant, with five working farms continuing to give the place a rural air.

This view of Carlton village, published by Raynor of Barnsley and probably taken on a quiet Sunday afternoon in about 1905, helps us to appreciate the rural nature of life at the heart of small villages despite the close proximity of major collieries. The two fashionable ladies, one pushing a bicycle, strolling in the middle of the road and what appears to be a mother and daughter add human interest to the scene. Farm buildings can be seen stretching along one side of the main street, and the stump of the village cross is just visible at the crossroads. Across from the relatively new church is the Sunday School room. The church is clearly a majestic building within this tranquil setting. (*Old Barnsley*)

This photograph was taken from almost the same position as the above but about fifteen years later, *c.* 1918. New buildings now occupy the corner by the junction including Samuel Barrowclough's newsagency and post office. The well-dressed lady on the causeway adds interest to the scene, as does the more elderly woman across the road, who appears to be curious about a photographer who had positioned himself in the middle of the road despite the approaching vehicle. (*Old Barnsley*)

The attractive cover of the parish magazine for February 1949, towards the end of Ernest Ashmore's ministry. With the development of large housing estates at Athersley and New Lodge – in the distant and hitherto 'empty' western part of the parish – services had had to be held in a wooden structure (dedicated to St Helen), but a new church was subsequently built on Laithes Lane in 1954. By 1973 St Helen's functioned as an independent parish.

The interior of St John's from a picture postcard posted in Carlton in November 1906. The sender, 'AB', informs 'Maggie' of Wakefield that 'it was taken with the Easter decorations' on show. The paraffin lights shown in the photograph were soon superseded by gas, which was introduced into the village in 1904.

Carlton village from the top of Wharncliffe Woodmoor (1,2 &3) 'muckstack' in 1969, showing houses, streets and terraces that developed close to the pit. In the near foreground are allotments adjoining the end of Bramah Street, formerly Chapman's Row/Bramah Row, in an area also known as The Roost or Rogues Roost.

Mr and Mrs Goodier outside their cottage, 9 Royston Lane, formerly 'known by the sign of' the Shoulder of Mutton, c. 1973. The alehouse/pub has a long association with the Walker family, probably going back to the seventeenth century when Carlton was admonished in the Quarter Sessions for having too many drinking places 'for such a small place', 'two being sufficient'. Elizabeth Walker carried on the business following the death of her husband John, in about 1839, and after her death the licence passed to her daughters Elizabeth and Mary. Their long association resulted in the premises being known locally as Old Maids' Cottages, and the adjacent lane (now Cronkhill Lane) as Old Maids' Lane.

Grays Road, when the colliery spoil heap was still a prominent feature, mid-1970s. In the 1950s small groups of the terraced properties were owned by private landlords, who rented them to miners' families. At the bottom of the street was a fried fish shop and, at the junction with Crookes Lane, Rushton's corner shop. Another small shop – Lomas's (previously Murrays and Atkinson's) – occupied a house in the middle of the left-hand terrace; and there was yet another fried fish shop near the top of the street (Goodlad's). The wall at the Wood Lane end of the street was locally known as 'spent up corner' where miners passed the time of day by having a smoke and chat.

In December 1871 Joshua Willey, an enterprising Hoyland shopkeeper, advertised the opening of a new colliery on Lord Wharncliffe's estate at Carlton, able to supply customers with 'best house coal for 7s a ton'. The Woodmoor Seam – 3 ft thick and of good quality – had been reached on 26 October 1871 at a depth of just over 40 yards. Two days later Mr and Mrs Willey and their two sons Joseph and John celebrated the extraction of the first coal by carting it in triumph from Carlton to Hoyland, where they were met by Hoyland Brass Band playing 'See the Conquering Hero Comes'. The Willeys were bought out in 1873/4 by a new company with capital of £20,000, but

the pit, now with four shafts, was bought back for £18,000 by Willey at an auction in 1876. Within a few years Henry Aston Allport of Dodworth, whose father managed the Great Midland Railway, was paying the coal rents. In 1883 the private pit was converted in name and substance into the Wharncliffe Woodmoor Colliery Company, employing about 330 persons, but sold in 1916 to Sir Joseph Hewitt. On Joseph's death in 1923 Wharncliffe Woodmoor became part of the Sutherland family's considerable colliery interests. Sam Diggle was the general manager during the Hewitt and Sutherland ownership.

A studio photograph of some of the Willey family and associates, *c.* 1890. Joseph/Josey Willey in the centre, his hand on the dog, was a chemist and druggist in Hoyland. Joshua Willey (*c.* 1823–91), mining entrepreneur and father of Joseph, resided at Carlton House in the village. (*Miss W. Waton*)

'Cum on lass, there's been an accident at t' top pit' were the words used by the father of trainee nurse Eleanor Caswell to awaken her in the early hours of 6 August 1936. Mr Caswell was a member of the pit rescue team. Distressing scenes at the pit head were front-page news in regional and national newspapers, as can be seen in this example. Eleanor, aged nineteen, assisted local doctor Hector Henderson and worked alongside midwife Mrs Bateman. The early signs proved to be both ominous and depressing: 'We saw rescue workers going in with canaries and bringing them out dead so we knew what to expect.' Some fifty-seven men died instantly following an explosion, either from the blast or from carbon monoxide poisoning. The writer's father, then a young man aged seventeen, worked at the pit, but fortunately was not on duty at the time of the accident.

Four miners (underground fitters) in the pit yard at the NCB Wharncliffe Woodmoor 1, 2 and 3 colliery, *c* 1960. They are, left to right, Ken Jones, Keith Jones, Fred Elliott and Brian Summerfield. The pit finally closed on 16 August 1966, twenty-nine years after nationalisation. Its sister pit was to outlive it by four years, after which Carlton was no longer (at least economically) a mining village.

Two men appear to be undertaking remedial work on the roof of Carlton Co-op and a dog sniffs by the gate of Carlton Villa on an otherwise deserted Church Street, *c.* 1910. Part of the outbuildings of Ivy Farm can be seen opposite Spring Lane school. (*Old Barnsley*)

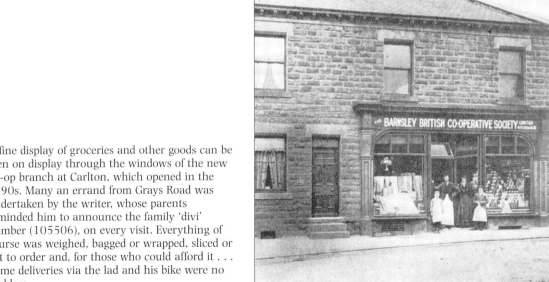

A fine display of groceries and other goods can be seen on display through the windows of the new Co-op branch at Carlton, which opened in the 1890s. Many an errand from Grays Road was undertaken by the writer, whose parents reminded him to announce the family 'divi' number (105506), on every visit. Everything of course was weighed, bagged or wrapped, sliced or cut to order and, for those who could afford it . . . home deliveries via the lad and his bike were no problem.

After its closure the Carlton Co-op building was used for the sale of second-hand furniture. The original façade remained intact, as can be seen in this photograph taken in January 1972. Part of the old school canteen is also in view. Today the old Co-op building has a modern frontage, and houses the Alternative Healing Centre.

A view of Church Street at the junction with Shaw Lane, c. 1972. It provides us with a good picture of the main barn of Brown's (Ivy) Farm which was demolished to make way for new housing a few years later. Brown's small butcher's shop can also be seen as part of the single-storey group of buildings attached to the barn. Brown's also bottled and sold their own milk, as well as probably supplying the Co-operative dairy: note the churns at the wall 'collecting point'.

Manor House Farm, despite the listed status, was in some danger of demolition when it was abandoned to the weather and ravaged by vandals in the mid-1980s. This photograph dates from a decade earlier when the farm was worked by the Richmond family. Residential conversion has thankfully rescued the main farmhouse, though the extended wing and some outbuildings have been lost.

Barnsley, 23rd March, 1870.

CARLTON, NEAR BARNSLEY.—TO BE LET BY TENDER, all that very desirable FARM, known by the name of the "Manor House Farm,' containing by recent survey about 418 acres of Arable, Meadow, and Pasture Land, to be entered upon at Lady-day next. This Farm has been in the occupation of Mr. Stocks (now retiring from farming pursuits) and his family for upwards of half a century.—Applications to view the Farm may be made to Mr. Stocks, on the premises, who will direct a person to show the same. Further particulars may be had of Mr. J. J. Smith, Estates Office, Wortley, Sheffield. Tenders for the same, with references as to respectability and responsibility, must be addressed to J. Wells, Esq, Toolbfersy House, Howden, Yorkshire, not later than the 10th of January, 1871. The highest Tender will not necessarily be accepted.

A sale letting notice for Manor House Farm, issued by the Wharncliffe estate to local newspapers in March 1870, following the retirement of Mr Stocks after 'upwards of half a century' of farming.

An understandably deserted-looking Wharncliffe Woodmoor 4 and 5 colliery (formerly owned by the Carlton Main Colliery Company Ltd), photographed just before its demolition in 1970. The first sod was ceremonially turned by the Earl of Wharncliffe at 2 pm on 12 November 1873 – no doubt in the presence of lessee Joshua Willey who sub-let to the Yorkshire and Derbyshire Iron and Coal Company; but sinking did not commence until 31 August 1874, the work proceeding slowly because of 'many difficulties', though accomplished 'without accident or injury'. The Barnsley Thick seam was reached via the no. 2 shaft at a depth of 290 yards, and this was duly celebrated by a dinner in the Wharncliffe Hotel.

By May 1878 the Yorkshire and Derbyshire Iron and Coal Company had built sixty brick and twelve stone cottages close to the pit at a cost of £152 each, to accommodate 250 men and boys for a weekly rent of 4s 6d (stone) and 4s 3d (brick). By 1890 the row had been extended to a very long terrace of about eighty-five houses, with the convenience of a Working Men's Club (see page 123) at the top of the street. One can imagine the 'knocker–up' (in the days before everyone had an alarm clock) with his long pole, tapping on upstairs windows in the early hours of cold winter mornings. (*Old Barnsley*)

Long Row and Stone Row photographed from the pit yard in the summer of 1969, when a few properties were still occupied but demolition was imminent. Wharncliffe Woodmoor 4 and 5 colliery closed on 31 July 1970 and the whole of the row was also erased from the landscape, though certainly not from the memories of its former residents.

The backs of Stone Row on the same day, washing on the line across the tiny yard of what appears to be the last occupied house. These 'superior' properties were built for the pit officials, but one was also the home of Police Constable Wright.

Early landscaping work in progress during 1973 when the Wharncliffe Woodmoor 4 and 5 site was being transformed for the Lyons Group, so as to create 'the world's biggest cake factory'.

The modern main entrance to what is now Manor Bakeries, a name adopted from the former Manor House farm on the opposite side of Fish Dam Lane.

£15m cake factory to be biggest in world

By the time Lyons Bakery start production at their projected £15m factory at Carlton, near Barnsley, they should have solved a multitude of problems that would have daunted many less determined companies.

Yet, with refreshing directness, the team who are planning the move north from the bakery's headquarters in South London admit the biggest question of all could remain unanswered until the plant is actually operational about Easter 1974.

What will it be like to work in the world's biggest cake factory? How will upwards of 1,700 people take to the atmosphere of one vast, open-plan shop-floor covering as much ground as the whole of Bramall Lane football and cricket ground — stands included?

There's no reason why they should know all the answers, of course.

Lyons' management have never experienced conditions like these and neither has anyone else in the cake-making business, not on the scale of £30m worth a year from a single plant.

There are good reasons, though, for supposing that if any company can successfully solve all the technical and human problems of a scheme like that at Carlton it'll be Lyons Bakery.

Competitions

Their financial record since Yorkshire-born Arthur Stocks took over as managing director three years ago has been little short of remarkable: losses have become profits, turnover has increased by 50 per cent in the last three years.

They've put themselves out in front of their many competitors with about 27½ per cent of the total package cake market in this country and that's more than double the share of any other single brand.

From the outset their approach to the Carlton project has been highly professional. They have left little to chance.

Perhaps two thousand people will lose their jobs when the Cadby Hall factory in London and other plants at Smethwick and Hove shut down and some production at Glasgow is transferred.

But Lyons have been looking closely to their welfare as they will be to the men and women they will eventually recruit from the Barnsley area.

Alternative jobs elsewhere in the Lyons group will be offered to employees with more than two years service when the move was announced.

And for the 150 key personnel they hope will transfer to Yorkshire there'll be financial help and paid visits to the area for househunting.

If there is still going to be some hardship that cannot be minimised by Lyons' determined management. Arthur Stocks accepts it as an unavoidable facet of taking Lyons Bakery out of a multi-storey, old-fashioned building with all its limitations on movement.

The new factory buildings at Carlton will cover about eight acres of a 65-acre site and under one roof flow-line production units will turn out more quickly and economically millions of fruit pies and jam tarts and hundreds of thousands of swiss rolls each week.

Problem

The site, bounded by an old colliery, slag heaps and narrow roads, cut across by a winding canal, is by no means an ideal one.

Yet it was chosen out of a hundred or more possibilities, says managing director Stocks, because it was the only site big enough — at the right price.

north is mainly one of incurring a distribution penalty but we should recover that by reducing other costs.

"Besides, we now have a site which is not only big enough for present development but gives us plenty of scope for expansion," he points out.

The attitudes of local authorities and the National Coal Board, their readiness to co-operate in improving the site, in helping to make it the landscaped garden factory Lyons envisage, was another decisive factor.

Pits disappear

The coal mine will soon disappear, the slag heaps will be lowered and contoured as part of a 130-acre area landscaped with grass, trees and shrubs.

The canal that cuts across the site will be diverted and approach roads to the projected factory will be improved, putting the Lyons delivery fleet within a few miles of the M1.

The technical problems of building the factory remain and they're pretty frightening to the layman.

For, above all, the Lyons' designers are having to think as they work, keeping open their options on final design and plant until the last moment.

Part of a feature from the *Sheffield Morning Telegraph* in 1973 describing the 130 acre 'landscaped garden factory Lyons envisage' at Carlton. Within two years it was anticipated that 1,700 employees would be on site, producing £30 million-worth of cakes a year, notably fruit pies, jam tarts and swiss rolls.

The Welsh chapel on Carlton Lane, shown here shortly before its demolition in 1984, was opened on 6 July 1902. It was built at a cost of about £200 in response to the needs of a small but significant (about 200-strong) migrant community, in particular displaced mining families from Mostyn in North Wales who were drawn to the village following the appointment of Evan Parry as a manager at Wharncliffe Woodmoor Colliery in 1884. (*Mel Jones*)

St Helen's Farm, photographed in February 1975, shortly before its demolition to make way for new housing. There were close links between this place and Monk Bretton Priory. A chapel was established here in the thirteenth century along with a prior's 'retiring house'. Near the farm was a holy well known to have been a place of pilgrimage, but as with similar sites it may have originated as a pagan shrine, 'Christianised' by the prefix of Saint and the addition of the letter H to Ellen. St Helen's may also have been the site of a substantial high status late medieval house, certainly associated with the Wortley family in the seventeenth century and replaced by one or more long lost fashionable buildings. One wonders how much might be revealed today in a 'Time Team' investigation!

CHAPTER FIVE

MONK BRETTON

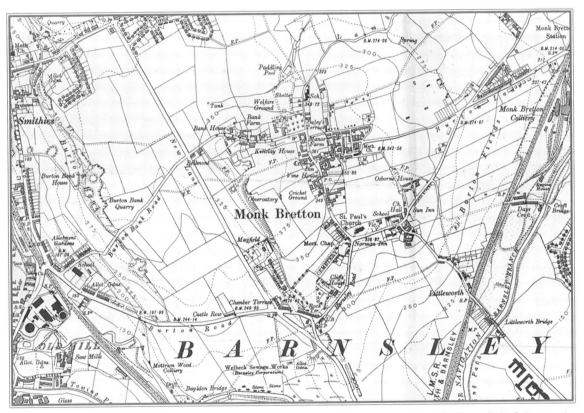

The 6 inch OS map of 1929 (revised 1938) helps us appreciate the hill-top setting of the old village of Monk Bretton (or Burton as it was formerly and alternatively called; the prefix Monk, from the nearby priory, distinguished it from West Bretton) overlooking the Dearne on its western side where, atop Burton Bank, the Victorian worthy the Rev. Mr Wordsworth erected his observatory, known locally as Monk Bretton Castle. We can see a cluster of buildings along Cross Street and High Street which form a link with Back Lane. This was the nucleus of the original Anglo-Saxon settlement. There was also early development along Westgate and at the top of Littleworth. A small Quaker burial ground (and later a meeting house), one of the first in the country, was strategically placed in an out of the way spot at the north end of Burton Bank, reached from Westgate, in about 1652. St Paul's church was sited at the south end of Cross Street in 1838 but replaced by a new building as early as 1876. Monk Bretton was a small rural community though in the early nineteenth century, along with Barnsley, was a noted centre of linen manufacture, principally via domestic handlooms. Monk Bretton Colliery, sunk in 1867–70 in the far eastern part of the township, did not have a significant impact on the form and character of the old village.

A well-trod path can be seen leading to The Castle via the pillars of the village First World War memorial. The roof of the club house of Monk Bretton Cricket Club is just in view on the left; and part of the Pheasant Inn on the right. The Castle, which came to life during royal celebrations and festivities, was unfortunately demolished in the 1960s. The memorial has now been moved across the road.

An interesting glimpse of the old village centre, the cross a focal point at the junction with High Street. Strictly speaking it was not a Butter Cross, since Monk Bretton was never granted market status because of its proximity to Barnsley. A series of village and wayside crosses were, however, once common in this part of the West Riding but Monk Bretton's is one of the best preserved examples. The Pheasant Inn is on the left and Manor Farm in the distance. Behind the cross is the village shop, with what appears to be the shadowy figure of its owner, Mrs Hirst, peering through the doorway. Outside are tinplate posters advertising the latest products, such as Lyons Tea. The men and boy add interest to the scene, particularly the man and perambulator. The public telephone box, which would have been painted cream with red glazing bars, is of a type widely introduced to the modified design of Sir Gilbert Scott in 1929, so provides us with a guide to the dating of the photograph. (*Old Barnsley*)

A delightful view of children sitting on the steps of the village cross, the camera pointing in the direction of High Street, *c.* 1914. The relatively new (with fashionable bay window) Butcher's Arms can be seen in the distance; and just before it part of the so-called Garrison Houses. Alfred Albert was landlord at the Butcher's Arms. Most of the vernacular buildings in view date from the seventeenth to the early nineteenth century and would have been of considerable architectural and historic interest had they survived. The conversion of the shaft of the cross into a gas lamp may seem an incongruous usage, but it is of an elegant design and may have contributed to the protection and saving of this important local landmark. (*Don Walton*)

Monk Bretton Cross and High Street, February 2000. Part of the base of the building was being damaged through heavy vehicles making a left turn from the direction of Westgate into High Street, so in the 1980s bus drivers agreed to circle the cross from the right, to avoid further crumbling of the base. The electric lamp was installed in the 1960s at a time when the whole structure appears to have been moved slightly from 'mid-junction' in the direction of High Street.

The front of the Pheasant Inn (then a 'Whitbread house') and the cross, from the direction of High Street, on a cold day in April 1970. Miss Angela Banks is standing on the steps of the cross.

Manor Farm is a late seventeenth-century building of considerable architectural interest, its name underlining its historic importance, though the old manor house lay further along Cross Street. The Richmond family has a long association with the farm. I gave evidence at a public enquiry held in 1971, in support of farmer Robert Richmond (born 1898) and several local residents who wished to preserve the six-bay barn and other outbuildings rather than see them disappear under road improvement plans. Barnsley Council maintained that the buildings had 'little architectural interest'. Fortunately the inspector, following evidence presented from both sides and a site visit, ruled in favour of preservation.

A sketch plan showing Manor Farm and the barn and outbuildings (at the corner of Westgate) that were scheduled for demolition. The barn and outbuildings on their own are indeed of no significant architectural merit, but their demolition would been a great loss to the farmstead – which, like most other examples, has evolved through continuous occupation and change over several centuries.

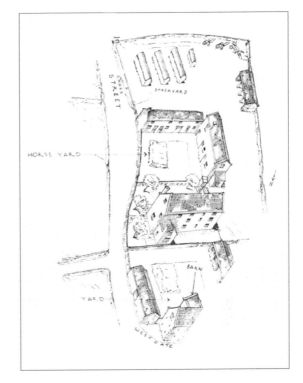

Relatively modern public buildings are always worthy of recording whilst they are still intact, unvandalised and in use, before builders or bulldozers arrive. This is Monk Bretton Miners' Welfare in 1970, built in red brick in 1931 towards the Burton Road end of Cross Street, quite close to St Paul's. Many people will have memories of sporting and social activities held in this modest-looking building which was of considerable community importance. A large modern house now occupies this site.

Part of Cross Street in about 1910, with stone farm buildings and houses on either side of a narrow road. Working farms in the village at this time included Vine Farm (Cross Street, Emmanuel Cherry), Manor Farm (William Richmond) and Cross Farm (William Robinson). John Parkin, publican of the Norman Inn, also farmed as did Arthur and George Peckett, William Livesey, Edward Burns and Joseph Priestley (the latter at Burton Bank). (*Old Barnsley*)

A contrasting view of Cross Street in October 1981. Hall Place, the new road on the right, takes its name from the demolished Hall Farm occupied from the sixteenth century by the Wood family. The tall farm building on the left is a late seventeenth- early eighteenth-century farm dovecote which survives as a listed building, now part of a modern complex of new and converted private housing (Dovecote Mews) at the former Cricket Farm. The couple on the pavement have just passed the small family butcher's shop of Mr R. Hall, previously Jack Watson's (see inset).

'Recruits Wanted!' proclaims the poster to the left of the central doorway of Monk Bretton post office, High Street (no. 26). This was for service at the time of the Boer War (1899–1902), since this postcard was sent in 1905. The postmaster shown here may have been William Hellewell, who was described as 'postmaster & stationer' when the First World War broke out. (*Old Barnsley*)

The former town hall, where the Monk Bretton Urban District Council met, was built as a school in 1821. It is shown on the left of this photograph, just before the demolition (*c.* 1969) of this group of buildings. To its right is the small Wesleyan Reform chapel, one of three Methodist chapels in the village. The town hall was re-used as a family health clinic. A new Methodist chapel was completed in 1963, a little lower down the street but on the opposite side of the road.

The Sun Inn is probably the oldest surviving public house in the old village. This is the then Barnsley Brewery pub when Thomas Randerson was landlord (see page 128), *c.* 1918. Four children and an old gentleman sit on a bench outside, whilst a lady peers hesitantly in the doorway. The high wall on the right forms part of the garden boundary of Osborne House. Note the marked bend in the road at this time, made perhaps even more pronounced by an extension to the left gable of the building. (*Old Barnsley*)

A more modern view, dating from October 1981 with 'John Smiths' and the Courage cockerel as the principal brewery signs. There is a bow window, a porch around the old doorway and the extension has gone, perhaps as part of the road alteration.

A fine view of Monk Bretton Colliery in its prime. The first coal was reached in July 1870 at a depth of 300 yards. Three shafts were eventually sunk. The Barnsley seam of coal here was of excellent quality, in great demand from the railway companies and for heavy industries such as iron- and steel-making. The colliery had ample branch lines which connected it to the Cudworth and Barnsley (LMSR) main line; and the Barnsley branch of the Aire and Calder Navigation (formerly the Barnsley Canal) ran by the pit. (*Old Barnsley*)

Monk Bretton Colliery finally closed in 1968. This view, from Burton Road looking across Burton Fields, dates from October 1971 when all the colliery buildings remained intact.

Children wait on the platform of Monk Bretton railway station, near Burton Road bridge. Note the gas lamps. The photographer is pointing his camera southwards in the direction of the colliery with the unmistakable chimney-stack of the upcast shaft. Major developments were to take place on land by the north side of the bridge during the post-war period, when Redfearns Bros of Harboro Hill Road, Old Mill, Barnsley, established a new glass-making factory. The local advantages of canal, railway, coal from the adjacent colliery and a site with plenty of room for expansion led the Old Mill site to close down in 1969, Monk Bretton developing into a major international plc. (*Old Barnsley*)

A lady with a small child pushes a pram along the uneven pavement of Burton Road, *c.* 1930. In the distance the road rises up the hill, terraced houses running along one side of most of its extent until a sharp bend is reached at the top leading on to Church Street. (The houses at the bend were demolished in about 1970.) The waste ground on the left of the photograph was where Castle Row was located. The road crossing the junction was at this time known as New Lane, and later Rotherham Road. (*Old Barnsley*)

CHAPTER SIX

SCHOOL DAYS

A class at Carlton Green Boys' School, c. 1927. Back row, left to right: Sam Wyatt, Mee, Jack Parkin, Fred Elliott, Roy McKenny, Harry Owen, Fred Wagstaffe, Jack Parry, White. Third row: Garnet Hodgson, Ernest Saxton, Walter Caswell, Joe Burton, Mavin, Bill Landen, Ken Bateman, -?-, Lionel Radford, -?-, -?-, Second row: Sammy Rowlands, Tom Hodgson, Bill Newman, Oscar Hold, Gordon Hall, Roy/George Kilner, Thompson, Frank Chambers, Royce Mckenny, Frank Harvey. Front row: Jeff Grayson, -?-, Butterfield, Fred Staves. Such photographs can be telling social documents. Four of the boys 'came prepared' wearing a shirt and tie, but the remaining thirty are less formally dressed. Perhaps this is not surprising bearing in mind the level of poverty in mining communities at this time, only a year or so after the great Coal Strike.

The first school in Carlton opened in 1877 at the edge of the village but close to the pit at Carlton Green. A Board School, it provided tuition for fifty-one mixed and infant children, but the first master, Henry Chadwick, commented in the log books about infrequent attendance because of illnesses such as measles, scarlet fever, diphtheria, whooping cough, influenza and typhoid; and of course coal strikes. In 1894 the school separated into boys' and girls' sections, a new extension having been built for the former. The school closed in 1934 but part of the building was used as a mortuary after the Carlton pit disaster of 1936. From 1945 to 1952 it was a factory of the Champion Scissors Company of Sheffield. The building was demolished two years later as part of road alterations and housing development but there are still vivid memories, including those of my father, of school days here more than seventy years ago. In this early photograph the master's house appears to dominate the view from Laithes Lane. (*Old Barnsley*)

Several mistresses of Carlton Green Board School or the Top School (to distinguish it from the new Infants' Department Board School at Spring Lane) outside the girls' entrance, late 1890s. Unmistakable is the huge 'flat cap' of the lady on the left. The headmistress was Miss Annie Walker. One of the women in the photograph is believed to be Miss Mary Brown. Being a 'Miss' was essential; in fact women teachers were required to resign if they married. Training for elementary teaching required only a period as a pupil teacher, though a few were able to finance college courses. (*Miss K. Parks*)

The Infants' School, at the top of Spring Lane, Carlton, shown here (centre, right) on an Edwardian picture postcard. The school opened in 1895 and was enlarged fifteen years later when it was described as 'Junior Mixed' and catered for 150 children under the headship of Miss Martha Ann Lodge. Part of the playground overlooked the gable end of the Co-operative branch shop, where flour stains are clearly visible near the first floor-loading bay.

Carlton Primary School, photographed during the demolition of the old buildings, 1972. Mining subsidence caused increasingly serious structural problems during the post-war period, though a new infants' extension was opened in 1953. In 1966 the Victorian/Edwardian wing closed down completely, junior children having to attend Burton Road School. A new primary school was eventually established, away from the heart of the village, on Fish Dam Lane in 1970, though a further extension in 1972 of the modern infants' building allowed it to function for several years as a nursery school. Many ex-pupils will recall the single-storey building in the playground being used as the school canteen and for occasional lessons and assemblies.

Carlton Primary School, class of 1949 (thirty-seven children). Back row, left to right: Marlene Watson, Peter Goodlad, Molly White, Pat Eastwood, Sid Lindley, Pat Slater, Pearl Vincent, Wilf Thackray, Sonia Beilby, Cynthia Harrison, Arthur Emmerson. Third row: Mrs Joan Deardon (assistant teacher), Anne Brookes, Brian Anglesea, Irene Hodgetts, John Bragger, Brenda Machen, Betty Shaw, Ken Eastwood, Cynthia Lever, Dave Timms, Wendy Bird, Roy Swift, Mrs Thomas (teacher). Second row: Mary Bamford, Brenda Farrar, Edwin Kilner, Glenys Jones, Sheila Neale, Alwyn Owen, Sally Houghton, Kathleen Newman, Fred Smith, Freda Landon, Carol Bolton. Front row: Ralph Iscotts, Neil Pickering, Brian Jones, Jimmy McLoughlin. (*Ken Eastwood*)

Classes were certainly large! Here, forty-seven pupils assemble for the school photographer in the playground of Carlton Primary School, *c.* 1937. Back row, left to right: Ernest Allen, Ernest Riley, George Robinson, -?-, Stanley Sevens, Kenneth Sevens, Betty Bamford, -?-, Vera Newman, Roy Chapman. Third row: Ester Newman, Margaret France, Ruby Land, David Hodgson, Derek Smith, Arnold Palmer, -?-, Hubert Morris, Peter Fox, Doreen Oliver, Edna Goddard, -?-, Arthur Riley, -?-, George Moat, -?-, -?-. Second row: -?-, Joan Bird, Michael Jones, Margaret Stewart, Mary Landon, -?-, Elsie Homer, -?-, Eileen Hold, Arthur Oakley, Len Saxton. Front row: Edward Campbell, Joyce Midgely, Mary Horbury, -?-, Joan Moxon, Sally White, Joan Elliott, -?-, Nora Ruse. (*Mrs M. Trepczyk, née France*)

Miss Parks's class at Carlton Primary School, late 1950s. Back row, left to right: Alan Biddle, -?-, -?-, -?-, -?-, Rimmington, Brian Jones, Kathleen Parks (teacher). Second row: -?-, -?-, Beechill, Donald Parkin, Trepczyk, -?-, Murrey, -?-, Jimmy Parkin. Front row: Janice Cooper, Marylin ? Holland, Gill, -?-, Vamplew, Robinson, Beechill, Sandra Elsworth. The photograph was taken by Brian Woodfine of Wombwell. Some of the lads are wearing 'snake belts' and ties, and all the girls have ribbons, summer dresses and sandals. Perhaps they were warned of the photographer's impending visit. Kathleen Parks taught at Carlton school (where her mother also taught) from 1939 until her retirement in 1977. Speaking to me in February 2000, she recalled that one of her infants' classes had fifty-nine pupils! (*Miss K. Parks*)

Staff at Carlton Primary School, *c.* 1955. Back row, left to right: Miss Tyas (Mrs Jones), Joan Deardon (assistant), Harry Roberts, Margaret Prest, Beryl Roberts. Front row: 'Betty' (Charlotte Elizabeth) Cook, Kathleen Alice Parks, Norman Holloway (headmaster), Mary Thomas, Rita Parkinson (Mrs Slater). (*Miss K. Parks*)

The smiling faces of Carlton Primary School football team, July 1958. Back row, left to right: Barker, Harry Roberts (teacher), Trevor Limbert, Parks, Brian Elliott, Alan Shirtcliffe, Alan Jones, Cooper. Second row: Arblaster, Gordon Shirtcliffe, John Holland (captain), Mervyn Grifiths, Donald Parkin. Front row: Naylor and Saxton. Brian Elliott was selected for Barnsley Junior Schools XL v. Scunthorpe Juniors at the Old Show Ground, Scunthorpe.

Carlton Primary School Cricket team, season 1949–50. Back row, left to right: Ralph Hisscox, Harry Roberts (teacher), Ron Burton, Alwyn Owen, John Bragger, Kenneth Hudson, Wilfred Thackray, Mr Taylor (teacher), Roy Swift; Middle row: Fred Smith, Ken Eastwood, Dave Timms, Peter Goodlad, Sid Lindley, Brian Anglesea, Arthur Emmerson. Front row: 'Corky' Allen, Brian Jones.Note the short trousers, braces and 'pumps' worn by some of the boys! (*Ken Eastwood*)

Royston Church School just before its demolition in the late 1970s. As a Public Elementary and 'National School' it was erected in 1844 and enlarged in 1889 to hold 410 children. In a directory of 1893 the school was 'shortly to be increased so as to hold 350 more [children]' when John Slack was master and Miss Caroline Witty infants' mistress, a very difficult year because of the miners' strike. Many children were absent because of 'bad boots or having none fit to put on'. Recalling the 1890s, in 1969 Mr J. Philips described the headmaster as 'a stern and scientific person wearing a mortar board hat, telling us not to rob birds' nests or we would be harshly dealt with'. In 1917 George Frederick Laycock was master and Miss Winifred Garrett infants' mistress. About five generations of Royston people attended this school, including my maternal grandmother.

Royston Church School gardening class, *c.* 1917. A school garden was established from about 1910, lessons scheduled on Monday and Thursday afternoons. The school received seven each of spades, forks, draw hoes, Dutch hoes and rakes. The subject was so successful that gardening appears to have been integrated with other lessons such as Arithmetic and English – so much for innovative Curriculum 2000!

Keep still and smile . . . Class 1, Royston Infants' class (forty-five children), Midland Road, 1934. Back row, left to right: Sutton, Gwen Peakman, Routledge, Gwyneth Cunliffe, Myrtle Churchill, Connie Wakefield, Howard Baker. Fourth row: -?-, Penny Parker, Roy Hayward, Rita Westnedge, -?-, -?-, -?-, Emily Taylor, Jessie Mitchell. Third row: Dorothy Preston, Donald Frear, -?-, Ray Hawkins, Doreen Brown, Harry Rodgers, Sam Greenfield, Glen Cunnah, -?-, Atkinson. Second row: Nicholson, Renee Law, Elaine Burton, Margaret Skidmore, Margaret Radley, Jenny Harrison, Lily Bettley, Vera Guest, Audrey Dyer. Front row: includes Possam, Joe Roberts, George Nell, Ben Smith, Joe Cole, Garret and Eccles. Miss Patterson (headmistress) is on the left and class teacher Miss Jones is on the right. (*Mrs A. Murdock*)

Royston Modern School had separate departments for boys and girls (11–15 years). Ten prefects and a teacher from the Boys' School are shown here in about 1955. Back row, left to right: Nev Taylor (teacher), Dennis Lowe, Cusworth, Don Wright. Front row: Cooke, Peter James, Trevor Spinks, Charlie Wilson, Colin Elstone, Malcolm McDonald, Cliff Everard. (*C. and M. Elstone*)

Netball team, Royston Secondary Modern School (Girls' Department), 1956–57. Back row, left to right: Pat Heaton (teacher), Pam Wooffindin, April Lloyd, Megan Wooffindin, Barbara Cooke, Miss F. Parker (headmistress); front row: Denise Beven, Valerie Cooper, Ann Bailey, -?-, Norma Standeven. (*C. and M. Elstone*)

Staff at Royston Modern School (Girls' Dept), *c.* 1956. Back row, left to right: Miss Jeanine Rostance, Miss Millie Longthorne, Miss Enid Russell, Miss Pat Heaton (now Mrs M. Buckle), German visitor, Mrs Crossley (Sec.). Front row: Miss Twigg, Miss Lappage, Miss Enid Binelli (now Mrs Brook), Miss F. Parker (headmistress), Miss Joyce Kirkby (now Mrs Handley), Miss Nora Websdale and Miss Molly Scott. (*C. and M. Elstone*)

A more informal photograph of staff at Royston Modern School (Girls') on a sunny day, with the school being painted in the background, *c.* 1952. Left to right: Joan Atkinson, Miss Parker (headmistress), Mrs B. Dyson, Mrs Gaynor Bamford, Mrs M. Websdale, Miss M. Hayes and Mrs Joyce Handley. (*Mrs G. Bamford*)

The cast of *The Rose of England*, one of a series of 1950s drama productions at Royston Modern School (Girls'). The photograph was taken by J.L. Wood. (*Mrs G. Bamford*)

J.L. Wood was also present in the new hall at Royston Modern School (Girls') about twenty years earlier in order to photograph the girls in a *c*. 1937 production that included this scene of 'Grecian dancers'. With a big smile on her face, Audrey Dyer née Murdock is on the extreme left of the stage. (*Mrs A. Murdock*)

Girls at Royston Modern School put on a popular production of *Little Women* in 1956–57. The cast included Megan Wooffindin, April Lloyd, Ann Caswell, Norma Standeven, Ann Simpson, Ann Merrels and Elaine Roebuck. (*C. and M. Elstone*)

The cast of *Little Women*, Royston Secondary Modern School (Girls'), 1956 or 1957. (*C. and M. Elstone*)

Royston Secondary Modern School Under 15s, shown here with teacher and coach Brian Elliott, had a successful season in 1973–4. Team members include Hudson (back row, second left), Smith (captain, front row, with trophy) and Dyer (right of Smith).

In 1979 a Jogging Club for students, staff and parents at Royston Comprehensive School was very popular. Its dual purpose was to participate in Fun Runs and raise money for charity. The tee-shirts and banner were designed by the pupils. Here the group are celebrating their recent appearance in the Sunday Times National Fun Run, held in Hyde Park, London, when Jimmy Savile gave over fifty of the group special public praise and they received a write-up in a national running magazine. Trailing at the back are staff Brian Elliott, Kath Horsfield, Carol Green, Megan Elstone and Ken Gomersall.

Members of Royston Comprehensive School Jogging Club present a cheque to the British Heart Foundation representative, following participation and sponsorship in the Humber Bridge Fun Run in 1982. The group was one of the first to run across the new bridge in an official event. Back row, left to right: Belinda Holliday, Lisa Jones, Leslie Dunderdale, Claire Street, Sarah Firth, Brian Elliott (teacher), Alison Thomas, Deborah Burton, Melanie Marshall. Front row: Greg Moxon, Deborah Winstanley, Joanne McDonald, Joanne Barker, BHF rep., Lee Brenton, Richard Sunman, Michael Sealey. Claire Crag is standing behind the three boys, front right.

Staff at Royston Comprehensive School, 1973–4. Back row, left to right: -?-, -?-, Brian Elliott, Ian Cooper, Dave Howdle, Colin Genloud, Ken Gomersall, Grant Smith, Jim Lodge, John O'Brien. Second row: Norman Pyke, Doreen Lancaster, Sandra Taylor, Olive Morte, Dorothy Skelly, -?-, Gillian Harris, Carol Green, Miss Fenny, Steve Hardacre. Front row: Graham Mounsey, Mary Schofield, Ron North, Colin Wilson (headmaster), Joyce Handley, John Murray, Jean Athay.

Looking very smart in their school uniform, Year 2, Mrs Watkins' class, Royston Church School, 1999. Back row, left to right: Mrs Chambers (NTA), Mathew Stirland, Leigh-Anne Lunn, Olivia Ellis, Abigail Limb, Matthew Lovitt, Benjamin Homer, Eve Walker, Samuel Winch, Craig Lunn, Mrs Watkins. Third row: Thomas Haigh, Luke Bridgewater, Todd Sweeney, Jennifer Phillips, Lewis Ellis, Luke Wilson, Joseph Whipp, Kimberley Shaw, Joshua Harris, James Haigh. Second row: Joshua Kay, Lauren Newton, Jacob Gill, Joshua Kaye, Nathan Turner, Luke Roberts, Thomas Oldroyd, Benjamin Wray, Joe Dransfield. Front row: Joanne Cassidy, Kimberley Douthwaite, Ebony Wheatley, Daniel Howison. In terms of appearance and dress this makes an interesting comparison with the old school photographs already shown.

There was a great deal of poverty in mining communities during the 1930s, especially when families were large. This photograph shows some of my aunts and an uncle. Left to right, they are Audrey (b. 1926), Ruby (b. 1925), Frank (b. 1931) and Joan (b. c.1928). They were four (of nine surviving) children of Fred (a coal miner) and Susannah Elliott née Firth. Wellington boots were convenient and cheap footwear for use in both winter and summer!

A similar group of miner's children, the girls wearing aprons. They are, left to right, Samuel, Ebenezer (b. 1904), May (seated) and Sarah Hawkes. The family lived at 19 Mason's Row, off Shaw Lane, Carlton. Samuel, who worked at Wharncliffe Woodmoor (4 and 5) colliery, was killed at the pit on Easter Monday, 1954. Ebenezer was to work at Grimethorpe colliery. (B. Hawkes)

Miner Fred Elliott (1888–1948) with his baby son, also named Fred (b. 1917), probably in 1918 outside Hilda Terrace, Carlton, within the shadow of the colliery spoil heap.

Children playing at a popular landmark known as The Round House, an octagonal lodge built to the design of the noted Yorkshire architect John Carr. It served New Lodge House, which was built for Colvin Clarke, Carr's nephew, in the late 1790s. The little girl standing by the window is Gloria Jackson. This rare photograph was taken just prior to the demolition of the lodge in the early 1950s.

CHAPTER SEVEN

CELEBRATION &
RECREATION

Barnsley's Regent Street Congregational Church Guild chose to hold their garden party at Monk Bretton on 17 June (a Thursday) in 1915, possibly in a member's garden at a pleasant hillside property called Mayfield. The backs of a distinctive landmark, Castle Row, a three-storey terrace of about ten cottages (also known as Salt Pie Houses) on Burton Road can be seen on the right of the photograph; the houses were named after the Castle folly on Burton Bank. The occasion must have been a welcome respite for the mainly officers and a few ranks shown in the photograph. One wonders how many in attendance here survived the first action of the Barnsley Pals, on 1 July 1916. (Old Barnsley)

This photograph was probably taken on 8 May 1945 on Victory in Europe Day (VE-Day) to commemorate the German surrender to the Allied forces, the end of the Second World War in Europe. Most of the children from Carlton respond very well to the photographer's instructions to wave Union flags and make the 'V' sign.

Despite the continuation of rationing impromptu street parties captured the euphoria of the immediate post-war era. There are plenty of smiling faces on this happy occasion, believed to be in July 1945, on land off High Street, Royston, opposite Wallace Arnold's (now Cobbys') and Mrs Wright's fish and chip shop. Note the air raid shelters in the background. The little girl seated on the orange box is Brenda Dale; behind her is Margaret Marshall (now Mrs Cooke). Others on and around this row of tables include Mrs Pearson, Ralph Pearson, Derek Grayson, Sheila White and Brian Wilson. On and around the left-hand row of tables are boys Mick Shaw and Albert Hemmings, adults Gwen Jackson (wearing berry hat), Nelly Jepson and Mrs Levitt. The lady standing at the back wearing a chain is Mrs Fisher. (*Mr and Mrs A. Cooke*)

Seventy-nine men of Carlton Home Guard assemble for a group photograph outside Carlton Green School, 1944. A number of the men were clearly First World War veterans including 'Jack' Skilton (sixth from right, second row from the front) who wrote a poem read at the 'stand down' farewell dinner which the men attended in 1945. Seventh and ninth from the left on the back row are Horace Breeze and Thomas Procter, now seventy-eight, who recalled the 'plane spotters used to congregate

on Woolley Edge and we used to congregate up there with guns to protect them'. Others in the photograph include Bill Brown (front row, second right), Bill Chambers (middle of front row, behind one of the trophies won for shooting), Tommy Cotton (far left, second row from front), and, not in any order, Second-Lieutenant Billy Nuttall, Lieutenants Ogley and Ellis, Company Commander Major Frank Green and his son Deplidge, Sergeant Major Alf Vaughan, Lieutenants Ferguson, Bennett, Coldwell, Cawthorne, Waring, Heathcote, Skirrow, and another First World War veteran, Tom Hughes. Joseph Ride is third from the left on the front row. The man in the helmet, back row extreme left, is Eric Simmons, a motor-cycle dispatch rider. (*Mrs W. Chambers*)

Flight Sergeant Roy Mason (Royston Flight) when he was a miner at Wharncliffe Woodmoor 4 and 5 Colliery, *c.* 1944. Royston Modern School, Midland Road, was HQ. After thirty-four years of parliamentary service including high offices of state, most notably as Secretary of State for Northern Ireland, Roy was honoured with a life peerage in 1987 and remains an active member of the House of Lords. (*Lord Mason of Barnsley*)

We must not forget that young women were also very much involved in war-time defence training. Here are thirty-nine smart-looking members of the Girls' Training Corp in one of the quads at Royston Secondary School in 1942. Miss Parker, headmistress of the girls' school, is seated, in uniform, in the centre of the front row. Several other teachers attended, including Winnie Gardener (back row, first on left) and Joan Atkinson, later Mrs McGougan (to the left of Miss Parker). Many of the girls were pupils at Normanton School, including Audrey Murdock, back row, fifth from right, who wasn't smiling despite the best efforts of photographer James Wood because she had just had some teeth extracted! (*Mrs A. Murdock*)

Gymnastics and 'health and strength' were very popular at Monckton Club and Institute, but here two locals are showing both strength and flexibility in a photographer's studio. The lower young man could be Royston-born Phil Clare who, despite his slight build, became famous for his amazing strongman feats. He was also a keen cyclist. (*Rosalie Bailey*)

Open-air parties were of course also held to celebrate royal occasions. This one is from Smithies, for the Coronation of Queen Elizabeth II in 1953. Councillor Trueman and his wife (holding a commemorative mug) can be seen on the right-hand side of the photograph. Others in the group include Turton, Bent and Cooke. The picture was taken in a field at the rear of Ridings Avenue. (*Mrs G. Bamford*)

Children at Carlton (Methodist?) Sunday School taking part in King George V's Silver Jubilee celebrations, 6 May 1935. Herbert Hall is on the back row, seventh from the right. Others include Edwin Jones, Percy Day, Walter Harrison, Ewart Lomas, Johnny Robinson, Herbert Powers, Henry Robinson, Mary Wilkinson, Olive Wilkinson, Gwendolene Raybold, Margaret Newman, Joyce Holmes, Audrey Bamforth, Betsy Beachall, Frank Elliott, Geoff Wagstaff, Ken Hall, Arnold Hall, Nora Ruse, Geoff Whitehouse and George Robinson.

Royston Wesleyan amateur football team and officials, *c* 1915. The forward with the football, probably the captain, is Monckton colliery worker William Dyer. Seated on the extreme right, wearing a flat cap, is Richard Murdock who migrated to Royston from Liverpool, finding work at the colliery as a timekeeper. The professional-looking trainer, with gloves and a towel over his shoulder, is Albert Key; seated next to him is Horn. Others on this photograph by J.L. Wood include Hall and, in suit and seated (without cap), Tommy Greenfield. Note the sturdy boots! (*Mrs A. Murdock*)

Royston Midland WMC football club, Alfred Street, *c.* 1909. This is a typical three-tier arrangement of goalkeeper flanked by two full-backs, on the next row three half-backs and five forwards seated at the front, but Warner Gothard's composition – or the cropping of the postcard image – denies us sight of the players' boots. Again the trainer has a towel over his left shoulder and there are smart looking officials; and note the size of the flat caps! Standing on the right-hand side, again with flat cap, is Richard Murdock. (*Mrs A. Murdock*)

An unusually informal photograph of the young players and attentive supporters of Castle Green Rovers football team, Monk Bretton, *c.* 1906. Here we have a very good view of the playing kit of period: long-sleeved buttoned-up shirts, long shorts held up by elasticated 'snake' buckle belts, dark woollen socks and studded leather boots.

The young footballers of Royston Dynamos Under 8s in their sponsored shirts are shown here at Royston High School field in 1999, quite a contrast to images of almost a century earlier. Back row, left to right: Ben Homer, Bradley Pickering, Jack Yates, Lewis Copeland, Mr Brian Pickering (coach), Danny Sammon, Danny Hennigan, Jacob Hill, Thomas Healey, Daniel Drake, Lewis Butcher. Front row: Craig Lunn, Joshua Kaye, Mathew Stirland, David Testkowski, Craig Bailey, Ashley Powers, Sam Winch, Luke Wilson and Jack Stores.

The photographer who took this superb image is not named but we know that it is of Wharncliffe Woodmoor [Colliery] Cricket Club, probably in Carlton Miners' Welfare Recreation Ground (Carlton park), *c.* 1925. Back row, left to right: G. Owen, T. Fletcher, A. Blakey, J. Helliwell, W. Chambers, R. Goodall. Second row: S. Fox, A. Jones, W. Clarkson. Front row: Clarence Cooke (kneeling), Walter Cook, L. Crawshaw (both seated) and F. Briggs (kneeling). The club played fixtures from at least 1894. (*Alan Cook*)

A novelty men versus women match entertained 'one of the largest crowds ever gathered on the cricket ground' in Royston Miners' Welfare Park, as part of 'Memorial Hall Week' in the summer of 1951. The men of the memorial committee batted left-handed and could reach only a derisory seventy-five runs in reply to the ladies' grand total of over a hundred. Gaynor Bamford, a physical training teacher at Royston Modern Girls' School knocked the men's bowling for forty-five before she was out. Gaynor (on the left) is shown here with her batting partner Mrs Marian Davies. Highlight of the evening entertainment was a series of exhibition boxing bouts by Monckton Men and Boys' Institute Boxing Club under Mr D. Grant's supervision. (*Mrs G. Bamford*)

John Henry ('Johnny') Weston, cricketer and village character. Johnny was born in Monk Bretton in about 1890, playing his first cricket match in 1904. From 1918 to 1928 he was club captain and groundsman. When he moved jobs from Monk Bretton to Monckton colliery he started playing for the Monckton team, usually as captain and opening bat. But he always retained contact with his home club and again became groundsman in 1932, a task that he carried out until the late 1960s. Johnny stopped playing cricket in 1945. As a young man he also played for the village football team and billiards for the Working Men's Club team. Sport was his great passion as a participant and as a spectator. He could even recall watching Barnsley FC in 1898 when they were newcomers to the Football League and never missed a game for fifty years. By 1970 he had not missed watching a Test Match in Yorkshire for sixty-eight years. Shortly before Johnny died, in the early 1970s, he was kind enough to take me on a guided tour of historic Monk Bretton. We finished up sitting under an old pear tree in his back garden where he reminisced about being a 'Burton Lord' (because a seventeenth-century Act of Parliament gave all freeholders manorial rights).

Syd Johnson was another legendary village cricketer, renowned for his cunning left-arm spin bowling and sporting longevity. A bachelor, Syd was born in Monk Terrace (Pit Row) in 1899 and joined Monk Bretton Cricket Club at the age of thirteen. He was still taking wickets in the Yorkshire Council at the age of seventy-two! His statistical record is amazing, including ten wickets in one innings on three occasions (e.g. 10 for 17 versus Darton in the 1930s); in the 1936 season he achieved a hundred wickets for an average of just five runs, and, though never a recognised batsman, hit six centuries. The writer saw Syd playing cricket at Monk Bretton towards the end of his long career and enjoyed occasional pavilion chats with him and of course his old friend Johnny Weston. Syd Johnson worked at the pit, was a milkman and railway worker during the war, leaving a considerable estate on his death, aged eighty-nine, in 1988.

Members, judges and officials of Royston and District Canine Society whose Show was held at the Ship Hotel on Saturday 28 January 1928. Mr Leonard Ashton, founder, show organiser and Honorary Secretary, is standing sixth from the right on the back row. Mr Ashton was also Secretary of the Monckton Athletic Sports Club. He was the son of a famous dog judge from Leeds, responsible for breeding the wire-haired terrier. Leonard Ashton's daughter Edna is seated on the far right of the photograph. Others include Dr T.G.A. Sweetman (third from left, standing) and Fred Swann (centre, standing). The alsation was a trained guide dog for the blind, one of the first in the country. The show attracted entries from a wide area including Barnsley, Sheffield, Rotherham and Doncaster, but the shortage of entries from local working miners was said, by Mr Ashton, to be not simply because of the expense but the amount of preparation time needed to get the animal into top-class condition, and administrative delays in allocating prize money. (*Rosalie Bailey*)

Royston New Monckton Colliery Institute Band at the side of the Palace cinema, 1946. It was formerly known as the Home Guard Band and previously Royston Subscription Prize Band, and was formed in 1904. Back row, left to right: Gerald Reaney, Albert Woolhouse, Ralph Hackett, Roy Oakley, James, Roy Brown, Frank Heaton, Fred Ogley, Albert Hackett, -?-. Second row: Mr Moorhouse, Ossie Brier, Roy Jones,-?-, Ron Cox, Horace Hayward, Roy Beddows, Bill Green, Oliver Hindmarsh, Reg Emery, Max Wood, Walt Blakeley, Charlie Woolhouse Jnr, Jimmy Greenfield. Front row: Tom Pickles, Colin Wagstaff, Reg Wray, Cleasby Green, George Green (father of Bill), William Foster (conductor), Wally Fearn (president), Ray Cox, Roy Blakeley and Charlie Woolhouse Snr. Mr W. Foster had recently taken over the conductorship after notable experience with the famous Grimethorpe Colliery Band. (*D. Hindmarsh, W. Green and R. Brown*)

There were some changes of personnel when the Royston NMCI band was photographed on the stage in Royston Secondary School in 1948. They were the first band to win a large new championship trophy (centre stage) in a recent contest at the City Hall, Sheffield. Back row, left to right: Colin Butterwood, Roy Beddows, Pearson, -?-, Roy Brown, Peter James, Mr Gill (colliery manager), Wally Fearn (president), and Dennis Beddows. Second row: Horace Heaton, Albert Woolhouse, Frank Heaton, Hill, Gerald Reaney, Ron Cox, William Foster (conductor), Horace Hayward, Roy Jones, Phil Robinson, Walter Blakeley, Sam Vamplew and George Green. Front row: Lewis Cox, Colin Wagstaff, Ray Cox, Oliver Hindmarsh, Bill Green, Reg Emery, Reg Wray, Cleasby Green, Sam Musgreaves, Roy Blakeley, -?-, Roy Brown recalls that they were wearing converted ex-police uniforms! Two years later, in August 1950, the band made a live BBC Home Service radio broadcast in the 'Industry Entertains' series. (*D. Hindmarsh, W. Green and R. Brown*)

Oliver Hindmarsh, aged about ten outside terraced house 3 Whincover, Royston, *c.* 1920. These canalside properties were built by Cutts, a well-known local family of builders and undertakers who in a directory of 1893 were described as 'joiners' and having 'saw mills'. The houses were demolished in about 1938. Oliver played euphonium in the village brassband until his mid-seventies. (*D. Hindmarsh*)

The Royston Carnival was always a popular occasion, held at a number of open-air venues. This example dates from the Silver Jubilee year of 1935 when it was in the Board School field, off Midland Road. James L. Wood was of course present to record appropriate scenes, including this prize-winning float entered by the British Legion. Audrey Murdock (née Dyer) was the Angel of Peace and a wounded soldier can be seen on the dray and pony, probably provided by Mr Walshaw of Strawberry Gardens. First World War memories were of course still fresh in the minds of most families. (*Mrs A. Murdock*)

Royston Church Gala was held in 'Garnham's Field' behind the Packhorse Hotel in May 1983. In the photograph we can see Father John Hudson and Rosalie Bailey and, seated at the drums, Barnsley District Mayor Councillor Ken Rispin, a bachelor who chose Royston Infants' School headmistress Mrs Shelagh Hayward as his Mayoral partner. Ken, a former railwayman and D-Day veteran, was said to be the first Royston-born Mayor of Barnsley. He died aged seventy-five in 1993. (*Rosalie Bailey*)

Keeping an allotment was of course a very popular recreational activity, and families benefited from fresh produce. This photograph, dating from about 1940, shows Samuel Hawkes and his dog Mick on his allotment off Shaw Lane, Carlton. Samuel worked at the nearby Carlton Main (Wharncliffe Woodmoor 4 and 5) colliery. (*B. Hawkes*)

Samuel Hawkes would have known Carlton Main Club (est.1889–90) located at the end of Long Row (Carlton Terrace), here shown in 1969 shortly before demolition. The club secretary in 1910 was John Slack when there was a membership of 460. He was probably succeeded by Mr J. J. Whittaker who is listed in a directory of 1917. Thomas Mann was secretary in 1936.

Euphonium player and Royston NMC band member Bill Green aged seventeen, at his home, 26 Park Crescent, Royston, 1948. (*Bill Green*)

Veteran conductor/bandmaster of Royston Subscription Prize Band Mr George Buckle, *c.* 1930. Note the baton and the fashion detail of his coat. This is a fine studio photograph by J.L. Wood. (*D. Hindmarsh*)

ROYSTON HOSPITAL SUNDAY

(IN AID OF THE BECKETT HOSPITAL, BARNSLEY).

↩ A PROCESSION ↪

Of the various Lodges and Friendly Societies, together with the Members and Scholars of the Sunday Schools of the District, will take place

On SUNDAY, AUGUST 28th, 1921,

The Procession, headed by the **Royston Subscription Prize Band**, will meet all Friendly Societies at the "Wells," starting at 1-30 p.m., and proceed by way of High Street, Midland Road, meeting all the Sunday School Scholars, along with the **Salvation Army Band**, and from there proceed to the "Midland Club" Field (kindly lent for the occasion by the Committee), where a

GRAND OPEN-AIR

Musical ✠ Festival

Will be held.   TO COMMENCE AT 3 o'clock.

SELECTIONS from HANDEL'S MESSIAH,

Will be performed by a Full Band, Chorus and 1000 children.

CONDUCTOR	- -	MR. A. KNIGHTON.
PIANIST	- -	MR. A. TRUELOVE.

SELECTION BY ROYSTON SUBSCRIPTION BAND.

Chair to be taken by Councillor G. A. GRIFFITHS, J.P.

ADDRESSES WILL BE DELIVERED BY

Mr. HERBERT SMITH, President Yorkshire Miners' Association, and

Mr. JOHN BUCKLE, Royston.

The Procession of the various Sunday Schools, headed by the Salvation Army Brass Band, will be in the following order:—1st, Salvation Army ; 2nd, Church of England ; 3rd, Wesleyan ; 4th, Primitives ; 5th, Monckton Primitives.

OFFERTORY BOXES AND SHEETS will be placed at all points for Collection, and the Committee trust the Public will give that generous support the Movement deserves.

Motors will run from Barnsley and Staincross, leaving Peel Square, Barnsley, at 2-15 and Staincross at 2-30 p.m.

Refreshments will be provided in the Midland Club for those from a distance who take part in the Concert.

PROGRAMMES - TWOPENCE EACH.

ROYSTON SUBSCRIPTION PRIZE BAND will give a **SACRED CONCERT** in the Midland Field in the Evening at 7-30 p.m.

President : Coun. T. H. Andrews,	Vice-President : Mr. E. Willets,
Hon. Secretary : Mr. H. Swallow,	Hon. Treasurer : Mr G. W. Westwood.

Royston's Subscription Prize Band and Salvation Army Band featured in a grand 'Hospital Sunday' fund-raising day of 28 August 1921, as can be seen by the splendid front cover of the official programme. Such events attracted thousands of participants and large crowds.

A centenary service for the consecration of St John the Evangelist's church, Carlton, August 1981. Here the procession approaches the entrance to the building, led by choir members. In their midst, behind the priest, is veteran lay-reader Elias Jones. At the rear is the parish priest the Rev. Peter Schofield, who produced a commemorative guide and short history of Carlton to mark the occasion. Churchwarden Irene Riley is also just visible at the rear. (*Miss K. Parks*)

A group photograph of the 1st Royston Girls' Brigade in Midland Road Methodist Church Hall, 1988. In the centre (third row from the front) is Mrs Gaynor Bamford (b. 1923) who had just 'retired' after fifty-one years' continuous service. When Gaynor married and moved to Royston the local Brigade was in danger of closure but, supported by her husband Randolf, she took over as Captain and by 1971 was Commissioner of the Division. (*Mrs G. Bamford*)

An impressive gathering of Royston worthies in the vicarage garden, *c* 1896. It is one of the oldest photographs in this collection. The occasion is believed to be a celebration of the successful funding of a new church clock. Ladies' fashions help to confirm the date: blouses (plain white or patterned) and a simple full-length skirt were just becoming more popular in contrast to the black attire of the older women. The monstrous hats are also typical of the late Victorian/early Edwardian era. All the party look quite glum, but this large composition of babies and adults must have been a considerable test for the photographer who probably used one of the older plate cameras, but equally, the occasion tested the patience of the group who would have been told to keep still for several minutes and for several exposures. Some in the group, notably churchwarden George Frobisher (in bowler hat, seated extreme left) look decidedly fed up, and one or two ladies look downright annoyed. The vicar is believed to be the Revd Robert John Thorpe who was incumbent from 1891 to 1911. Fourth from the left, seated, is Mrs Annie Cutts (née Hill). (*D. Hindmarsh*)

An assembly of Monk Bretton miners and their families, accompanied by a brass band outside the Sun Inn at Monk Bretton when Thomas Randerson held the licence, *c.* 1905. Mr Randerson is standing in front of the trade union banner, in shirt sleeves. His predecessor, Herbert Wood suffered embarrassment in 1892 when he 'hired' a group of local miners to collect a drayload of beer from Barnsley Brewery. Coincidentally, a meeting of Monk Bretton miners in the Three Cranes public house in Barnsley got wind of the affair, attacked the dray in Regent Street and consumed most of the contents of the casks, much to the disgust of the hired men who had been promised a complimentary barrel by the landlord!

Monk Bretton Ladies' football team played in the Barnsley Ladies League, losing the championship to Honeywell Ladies in the last match of the 1926/7 season. The team was founded by local shopkeeper and Labour councillor Joseph Henry Dodd, shown on the right of the photograph. His daughter Freda was in the team, which was formed to help raise funds for poor families during the 1926 General Strike. In 1993 Mrs Stoner (née Dodd, born 1909) recalled that matches were played 'in a real carnival atmosphere with a jazz band playing before we kicked off'. Most of the women wore hairnets because of the length of their hair. The trainer, standing on the left, pipe in hand, is Frank Myers, whose parents had nine sons and four daughters – enough for a mixed football team and two reserves.